MONEY

There is gold and a multitude of rubies
But more precious are the lips of knowledge.

PROVERBS 20:15

MONEY

Fifth and Revised Edition

LAWRENCE S. RITTER

&

WILLIAM L. SILBER

Basic Books, Inc., Publishers

NEW YORK

Library of Congress Catatloging in Publication Data

Ritter, Lawrence S.
 Money.

 Bibliography: p. 289
 Includes index.
 1. Money—United States. 2. Monetary policy—United
States. 3. Money. I. Silber, William L. II. Title.
HG540.R57 1984   332.4   83–45252
ISBN 0–465–04721–1
ISBN 0–465–04722–X (pbk.)

FOR

Bella and Irving Ritter

AND

Lillian F. Silber

a mother, a father,

and a wife,

all of whom deserve their share

of the blame

CONTENTS

PART I

IN THE BEGINNING

PART II

THE POWER OF THE PURSE

PART III

FEDERAL RESERVE POLICY MAKING

PART IV

FISCAL POLICY AND DEBT MANAGEMENT

PART V

OF STOCKS AND INTERMEDIARIES

PART VI

MONEY AND NATIONAL PRIORITIES

PART VII

INTERNATIONAL FINANCE

EPILOGUE

PART I

In the Beginning

1

A BOOK FOR THE CURIOUS

In 1931, Babe Ruth received a salary of $80,000 from the New York Yankees. His after-tax take-home pay was $68,-500. Today, many baseball players make $900,000 a year and, after taxes, take home about half that or $450,000. Are they really that much better off?

Actually, they are somewhat *worse* off! Consumer prices are now seven times higher than they were in 1931. At present prices, $450,000 can only buy what about $64,000 could buy in 1931. Babe Ruth's $68,500 was worth *more* in terms of purchasing power than $450,000 today!

All of which is not meant to prove that Babe Ruth was a better baseball player than the modern stars (which he was), but that inflation distorts economic relationships. Athletes making hundreds of thousands of dollars will make do, inflation or no inflation, but for most people rising prices are a more painful matter. As your income goes up, you may think you are earning more and moving up the ladder, but if prices are rising faster it is a mirage. You may be earning more dollars, but each dollar is worth less and less, so that after all is said and done you are no better (and maybe worse) off than you were before.

What does all this have to do with money? It is widely believed that increases in the price level are synonymous with increases in the money supply. The reason for this book is to explore precisely and thoroughly the influence of money on the economy. How it affects the price level, what it does to the volume of employment, whether it enhances or inhibits economic growth, and what role it plays in the attainment of national priorities. In short, this is a book about money and monetary policy.

Other questions also spring to mind. Is money responsible for the ups and downs of stock prices? Are high interest rates always bad? Is gold an essential part of our monetary system or a vestigial remnant of bygone days? Why do we now have floating exchange rates?

These questions have been highlighted in recent years by the rebirth of monetary policy as an instrument of national economic policy, and also by widely publicized debates between the Monetarists and the Keynesians. Monetarists are the standard-bearers of monetary policy and Keynesians the champions of fiscal policy. In recent years, for example, great controversy arose between them as to whether the economy could best be stabilized by exclusive reliance on monetary policy or by changes in tax rates and government spending, which are tools of fiscal policy.

We will explore the intricacies of money and monetary policy in the following way. Part I lays the foundations for understanding problems of the sort we have mentioned above. In particular, chapters 2 and 3 deal with the essentials of money and its relationship to the overall economy, and chapter 4 with the crucial debate between the Monetarists and the Keynesians. How does this theoretical confrontation lead to alternative policy recommendations for solving real-world problems?

Against this background, part II examines in detail the impact of monetary policy on the economy. How does it work? What effect does it have on the price level? What are some of the implications of high interest rates? Part III, in the same vein, explores the execution of monetary policy, including the mechanics of who pushes which levers at what times. Is there a better way to go about the whole business?

Having explored the execution and the effects of monetary policy, we return in part IV to the controversy between the Monetarists and the Keynesians, this time concentrating on the potentialities of fiscal policy. Is the policy split in the real world as deep as the ideological chasm that appears to separate these two groups?

Part V takes an in-depth look at some puzzling issues that swirl in the wake of both monetary and fiscal policy. Can knowledge of the intricacies of monetary policy help in forecasting the stock market? What is meant by financial intermediation and disintermediation?

Parts VI and VII explore two areas that have attracted widespread attention recently: national priorities and international finance (exchange rates, balance of payments deficits, gold, devaluation, and all that). It is said that only two men in the whole world really understand what international finance is all about—and they disagree. Finally, we end up with our crystal ball and try to fathom what money and the financial system might look like in the "Brave New World" of the twenty-first century.

This is not a long book. Perhaps it is even too short to do full justice to the ground it covers. Nevertheless, after you finish it, we hope you will be more informed about money and its role in economic life, and more capable of satisfying your curiosity about what is happening today and what is likely to happen tomorrow in the sphinx-like world of monetary policy.

2

ALL THAT GLITTERS

\

"The lack of money is the root of all evil," said George Bernard Shaw. While that might be somewhat of an exaggeration, there have been numerous periods in history when it appeared more true than false. There have also been rather lengthy episodes when the opposite seemed true: when economic disruption apparently stemmed not from too little money, but from too *much* of it.

From this line of thought, the question naturally arises: What is the "right" amount of money? Not too little, not too much, but just right. And how can we go about getting it?

Questions of this sort used to be considered heresy, back in the days when the economy was viewed as a marvel of perpetual motion, sparked by divine inspiration in the form of gold (which gave money intrinsic value) and human intelligence (which told us to stay out of the way and let things work out by themselves). Flanked by the twin eternal verities, the gold standard and the balanced budget, *laissez faire* reigned supreme. Let nature take its course, and everything will turn out for the best in this best of all possible worlds.

Today we are no longer so sure. Aggregate spending on the nation's output of new goods and services—the economy's gross national product (GNP)—is no longer seen as inevitably producing full employment, stable prices, a high rate of economic growth, balance in international payments, and all the other things we expect our economy to yield. We have experienced too many instances of GNP falling short of the mark, or overshooting it, to retain blind faith in any built-in self-correcting thermostat. So today we deliberately try to influence the course of economic events. We tinker, meddle, turn switches, push buttons, pull levers, and try to make things better.

But are they really any better? The answer is far from clear. Nevertheless, for most people the issue now is not *whether* the government should intervene, but how, when, and to what extent. The ends are not particularly new—high employment, price stability, economic growth, and balance of payments equilibrium—but the means are. The means most frequently used today to influence the economy's direction are *monetary policy* (the subject of this book) and *fiscal policy.* How well do they work? Are they appropriate to achieve their purposes? Can they be improved?

Very few people still equate paper money with rampant inflation, unbalanced budgets with creeping socialism, and Keynes with Marx. But the emotional content of the argument has not disappeared. It has merely moved next door— to the debate between the Monetarists and the Keynesians, between monetary policy versus fiscal policy, and to controversy over the execution of monetary policy.

As a first approximation, monetary policy involves regulating the money supply and conditions in financial markets in order to achieve the goals of national economic policy. Fiscal policy involves changing government spending and tax rates for similar purposes. We will return to fiscal policy later in the book. First, however, let us set the framework for our main concern—money and monetary policy.

The Supply of Money

How large a money supply should we have in the United States? What *is* money, anyway? And how much of it do we actually have?

Money is just what you think it is—what you spend when you want to buy something. The Indians used beads, Eskimos used fishhooks, and we use *currency* (coins and dollar bills) and, most of all, checking accounts (such as noninterest-bearing demand deposit accounts or interest-bearing NOW—negotiable order of withdrawal—accounts).

Money is used (1) as a means of payment, a medium of exchange, but it has other functions as well. It is also used (2) as a store of value, when people hold on to it, and (3) as a standard of value (a unit of account) when people compare prices and thereby assess relative values. But most prominently money is what you can spend, a generally acceptable medium of exchange that you can use to buy things or settle debts.

How much money do we actually have? It amounted to $500 billion in mid-1983, roughly $130 billion in the form of currency outside banks and $370 billion in checking accounts at banks and other financial institutions. However, the answer is not quite as simple as that, because there is more than one definition of what constitutes "money." This definition of money—currency outside banks plus checking accounts—is the most popular one, but it is not the only one.

Currency and checking accounts are spendable at face value virtually anywhere, at any time, so they are the most "liquid" assets a person can have. A liquid asset is something you can turn into the generally acceptable medium of exchange quickly without taking a loss—as compared with "frozen" assets, for example, which can be sold or liquidated on short notice only at a substantially lower price. Currency and checking accounts are the most liquid assets you can have (because they *are* the medium of exchange), but they are not the only liquid assets around. Government bonds are rather liquid, although you can't spend them. To spend them, you first have to exchange them for money. At the other extreme, real estate and vintage automobiles typically rank fairly low on the liquidity scale: If you have to sell quickly, you're likely to take a beating on the deal.

Thus liquidity is a continuum, ranging from currency and demand deposits at the top of the scale to a variety of frozen assets at the bottom. As a result, what we call "money" is not a fixed and immutable thing, like what we call water (H_2O), but to a great extent is a matter of judgment. There are several different definitions of money, each of which drops one notch lower on the liquidity scale in drawing the line between "money" and "all other assets."

Every week, for example, the *Wall Street Journal* and the *New York Times* report money supply data based on several different definitions of money. In fact, each definition has its own unique label, just like Campbell's soup or Heinz pickles.

The $500 billion money supply previously mentioned— currency plus checking accounts—is known as M1. Right behind it is M2, which drops a rung lower on the liquidity scale to include, among other things, such assets as passbook savings deposits, small-size time deposits, and money market accounts at commercial banks and thrift institutions, as well as shares in money market mutual funds. Time deposits are different from passbook savings deposits and money market accounts in that they have a scheduled maturity, such as six months or two years, and if you want to withdraw your funds earlier you suffer a substantial penalty by having to forfeit

part of the accumulated interest. Money market mutual
funds pool the funds of many small savers and invest in
high-yielding short-term assets; most of them permit their
shareholders to withdraw funds on demand. All these, plus
a few smaller items, summed to $1,500 billion in mid-1983;
added to the previous $500 billion yields a money supply
figure of $2,000 billion (M2).

M3 consists of M2 plus large-size ($100,000 and over) time
deposits at all depositary institutions. These amounted to
$300 billion in mid-1983, to make a grand total of $2,300
billion as the money supply (M3).

So what is the money supply in the United States? Is it
$500 billion (M1) or $2,300 billion (M3), or something in
between? Each definition of money has its adherents, but by
and large most economists prefer the simple definition of
money—M1—because it includes everything that is generally acceptable as a means of payment but no more. Once you
go beyond currency and checking accounts, it is hard to find
a logical place to stop, since many things (bonds, stocks,
waterbeds) contain liquidity in varying degree. Throughout
this book, therefore, we will for the most part stick to the first
definition of money (M1)—currency plus all checking accounts.

Now that we know what money is, a crucial question still
remains: *how much of it should there be?*

In theory, the answer is simple enough; presumably the
supply of money affects the rate of spending, and therefore
we should have enough money so that we buy, at current
prices, all the goods and services the economy is able to
produce. If we spend less, we will have idle capacity and idle
people. If we spend more, we will wind up with higher prices
but no more real goods or services. We need a money supply,

in other words, that is large enough to generate just the right amount of spending to give us a GNP that represents full employment at stable prices. More money than that would mean more spending and inflation, and less money would mean less spending and recession or depression.

In practice, unfortunately, the answer is not quite so simple. Precisely how much money will give us that much spending? The answer is not clear, because any given amount of money can conceivably be spent more or less rapidly, thereby generating a rather wide range of potential spending. In brief, the velocity of money, its rate of turnover, is as important as the supply. It is so important, in fact, that we will devote all of the next chapter to velocity and its implications.

Where, in all of this, does gold fit in? Regardless of what you might have heard, the amount of gold does *not* determine the money supply. Indeed, it has very little influence on it. In 1968, the last remaining link between the money supply and gold was severed, when a law requiring 25 percent gold backing behind most of our currency was repealed. If that is all news to you, it is a good indication of just how unimportant the connection between gold and money has always been, at least in our lifetime.

Both checking accounts and currency can be increased (or decreased) without any relation whatsoever to gold. Does that disturb you? Does it lead you to distrust the value of your money? Then send it to us. We'll be delighted to pay you ninety cents on the dollar, which should be a bargain if you believe all you read about a dollar being worth only sixty cents, or fifty cents, or whatever the latest figure might be.

If gold is not the watchdog, what is? What supervision is there over the creation (and destruction) of money? In other

words, who controls and formulates monetary policy? Before
we get into the details, let's back off for a moment and ask:
why all the fuss over money? What might the economy look
like without it?

The Importance of Money: Man Beats Barter

What good is money in the first place? In other words, why
was money invented (by Sir John Money in 3016 B.C.)?

For one thing, without money individuals in the economy
would have to devote more time to buying what they want
and selling what they don't. In other words, people would
have less time to work and play. A barter economy is one
without a medium of exchange or a unit of account (the
measuring rod function of money). Let's see what it might
be like in a barter economy.

Say you are a carpenter and agree to build a bookcase for
your neighbor, who happens to raise chickens and pays you
with four dozen eggs. You decide to keep a dozen for yourself, so you now have three dozen to exchange for the rest
of the week's groceries. All you must do is find a grocer who
is short of eggs.

What's more, you have to remember that a loaf of bread
exchanges for six eggs (it also exchanges for eleven books of
matches or three boxes of crayons or one Yankee Yearbook,
but never mind because you don't have any of these things
to spare). And of course all the other items on the grocer's
shelf have similar price tags—the tags are bigger than the
items.

Along comes money and simplifies matters. Workers are

paid in something called money, which they can then use to pay their bills and make their purchases (medium of exchange). We no longer need price tags giving rates of exchange between an item and everything else that might conceivably be exchanged for it. Instead, prices of goods and services are expressed in terms of money, a common denominator (unit of account).

The most important thing about the medium of exchange is that each and every person be confident that it can be passed on to someone else—that it be generally acceptable in trade. Paradoxically, a person will accept the medium of exchange only when certain that it can be passed on to someone else. One key characteristic is that the *uncertainty* over its value in trade must be very *low*. People will be more willing to accept the medium of exchange if they are certain what it is worth in terms of things they really want. The uncertainty of barter transactions makes people wary of exchange: if I want to sell my house and buy a car and you want to do just the reverse, we might be able to strike a deal except for the fact that you've got shifty eyes and are likely to rip me off by passing me a lemon. Hence no deal: I'm uncertain about the value of the thing I accept in exchange. The medium of exchange, which is handled often in many transactions, becomes familiar to us all and can be checked carefully for fraud, thereby reducing uncertainty in trading.

Closely related to the low-uncertainty-high-exchangeability characteristic is the ability to hold on to the medium of exchange without its deteriorating in value. It must be a good store of value. Otherwise, as soon as I accept the medium of exchange, I'll try to get rid of it, lest it be worth fewer and fewer goods and services tomorrow or the day after. If price inflation gets out of hand and I have little confidence that the medium of exchange will hold its value, I'll be reluctant to accept it in exchange; in other words, it won't be the medium of exchange for very long. This means we begin to slip back into barter, spending more time exchanging goods and less time producing, consuming and enjoying them.

The medium of exchange also usually serves as a unit of account. In other words, the prices of all other goods are expressed in terms of, say, dollars. Without such a unit of account, you'd have to remember the exchange ratios of soap for bread, knives for shirts, and bookcases for haircuts (and haircuts for soap). The unit of account reduces the information you have to carry around in your brain—freeing that limited space for creative speculation.

So money is a good thing. It frees people from spending too much time running around bartering goods and services, and allows them to undertake other endeavors—production, relaxation, contemplation, and temptation.

It is important to emphasize that people hold the medium of exchange—money—not because it has any intrinsic value but because it can be exchanged for things to eat, drink, wear, and play with. The *value* of a unit of money is determined, therefore, by the prices of each and every thing—more accurately, the average level of all prices. If prices go up, a unit of money (a dollar) is worth less because it will buy less; if prices go down—use your imagination—a dollar is worth more because it will buy more. So when we noted that the dollar was worth only fifty cents it meant simply that the dollar could now buy what fifty cents could have bought a few years ago (because prices have doubled).

What all this suggests is that the value of the dollar has nothing to do with gold or any other precious metal. And this reminds us to get back to the question of who determines how many dollars are floating around. As we might expect, this has something to do with the level of prices, inflation, and the "value of a dollar."

The Central Bank and Money Creation

The monetary authority in most countries is called the central bank. A central bank does not deal directly with the public; it is rather a bank for banks, and it is responsible for the execution of national monetary policy. In the United States the central bank is the Federal Reserve, created by Congress in 1913. It consists of twelve district Federal Reserve Banks, scattered throughout the country, and a Board of Governors in Washington. This hydra-headed monster, which some view as benign but others consider an ever-lurking peril, possesses ultimate authority over the money supply.

As noted previously, the money supply consists of currency and checking accounts. *Currency* is manufactured by money factories—the Bureau of Engraving and Printing and the Mint—and then shipped under rather heavy guard to the Treasury and the Federal Reserve for further distribution. For the most part it enters circulation when people and business firms cash checks at their local banks. Thus it is the public that ultimately decides what proportion of the money supply will be in the form of currency, with the Federal Reserve Banks wholesaling the necessary coins and paper to local banks. The Federal Reserve is not particularly concerned with the fraction of the money supply that is in one form or another, but rather with the *total* of demand deposits plus currency.

Most of the money supply (three-quarters of it) is in the form of checking accounts. Checking accounts in banks come into being when banks extend credit—that is, when they make loans or buy securities. Checking accounts vanish, as silently as they came, when banks contract credit—when bank loans are repaid or banks sell securities. It is precisely here, through its ability to control the behavior of banks, that the Federal Reserve wields its primary authority over the money supply and thereby implements monetary policy. This process of money creation by the banks under the influence of the Federal Reserve is sufficiently important and complex to deserve further explanation.

When a bank makes a loan to a consumer or business firm, it typically creates a checking account for the borrower's use. For example, when you borrow $1,000 from your friendly neighborhood bank, the bank will take your IOU and give you a checking account in return. From the commercial bank's point of view, it has an additional $1,000 of assets (namely, your IOU); this is matched by an additional $1,000 of liabilities (namely, your checking account). You could, of course, ask for $1,000 in $10 bills right then and there, stuff them in your pocket, and depart. But more likely you would be equally satisfied with the checking account, because by writing checks on it you can make payments just as well as with currency. The creation of this $1,000 in checking deposits means the money supply has increased by $1,000.

Similarly, when a bank buys a corporate or government bond, it pays for it by opening a checking account for the seller. Assume you are holding a $1,000 corporate or government bond in your investment portfolio, and you need cash. You might sell the bond to your local bank, which would then add $1,000 to your checking account. Once again, from the point of view of the bank, its assets (bonds) and liabilities (checking accounts) have gone up by $1,000. Just as by a bank loan, money has been created; the supply of money in the economy has increased by $1,000.

Conversely, when you repay a bank loan by giving the bank a check, the bank gives you back your IOU and at the same time lowers your deposit balance. If a bank sells a bond to an individual, the same reduction in deposits occurs. The supply of money declines. To repeat: banks create money (checking accounts) when they lend or buy securities, and destroy money when their loans are repaid or they sell securities.

Can they do this without limit? Is there any control over their ability to create and destroy money? No they can't and yes there is, and that is where the Federal Reserve comes into the picture.

A bank cannot always expand its checking account liabilities by making loans or buying securities. Banks are required by the Federal Reserve to hold reserves against their checking account liabilities—the current requirement is reserves of about 12 percent against checking deposits. *These reserves must be held in the form of vault cash or as a deposit in their regional Federal Reserve Bank.* Therefore, only if a bank has "excess" reserves, reserves over and above its requirements, can it create new checking deposits by making loans and buying securities.

Once a bank is "loaned up," with no more excess reserves, its ability to create money ceases. And if it has deficient reserves, not enough to support its existing deposits, the bank must somehow get additional reserves. Otherwise, it has no choice but to call in loans or sell securities in order to bring its deposits back in line with its reserves. If a bank has checking account deposits of $10,000 but only $1,100 in reserves, it would be $100 short of meeting its required reserves. One way to set itself right with the Federal Reserve would be to call in $834 worth of loans. This would reduce its deposits to $9,166, at which level its $1,100 of reserves satisfies the legal 12 percent requirement.

It is through the fulcrum of these reserves that the Federal Reserve influences bank lending and investing and thereby the money supply. The Federal Reserve manipulates the reserves of the banking system and the amount of checking accounts that they can support in several different ways.

In the first place, within prescribed limits established by Congress, the Federal Reserve can specify the reserve requirement percentage. Lowering the percentage, say from 12 to 10 percent, will instantly and automatically increase banks' excess reserves, enabling banks to make more loans (or buy securities) and to expand deposits. If reserve requirements were lowered from 12 to 10 percent, the bank with the $100 reserve deficiency would suddenly find itself with $100 in excess reserves. Raising the percentage, say to 15 percent, will just as quickly reduce excess reserves or create deficiencies, pressuring banks to call in loans (or sell securities), thereby reducing deposits.

Second, through facilities available for "discounting," member banks can temporarily borrow reserves from their regional Federal Reserve Bank at a price (the discount rate). For example, the problem bank, with checking accounts of $10,000 but only $1,100 in reserves, could avoid the embarrassment of having to call in loans if it were willing to borrow the needed $100 in reserves from its regional Federal Reserve Bank. The ability to borrow these reserves means that the money supply can remain unchanged. A bank could also take the initiative and borrow additional reserves to make *new* loans and thereby *increase* the money supply. The Fed-

eral Reserve influences the willingness of banks to borrow
reserves by manipulating the rate it charges on such loans.
A lower discount rate will tend to make borrowing reserves
more attractive to the commercial banks, and a higher rate
will tend to make it less attractive.

Third, and most important of all as a means of day-to-day
policy making, the Federal Reserve can buy or sell government securities (open market operations), thereby enlarging
or diminishing bank reserves. About $1,000 billion worth of
marketable government securities are held as investments by
the public—by individuals, corporations, financial institutions, and so on. These government securities came into
being when the United States Treasury had to borrow to
finance past budget deficits. Some are long-term bonds, running twenty or thirty years until maturity, and others are
shorter term, all the way down to government securities that
are issued for only a few months, called Treasury bills. The
existence of this pool of widely held marketable securities,
with many potential buyers and sellers, offers an ideal vehicle
through which the Federal Reserve can affect bank reserves.

When the Federal Reserve *buys* government securities in
the open market, much as you would buy a stock or a bond
on one of the stock exchanges, it pays for them with a check
drawn on itself. When the seller deposits that check in a
bank, and the bank presents the check to the Federal Reserve
for payment, the bank's deposits at the Federal Reserve Bank
—its reserves—increase. With more reserves, the bank can
make loans and increase its deposits.

Take the following concrete example. When the Federal
Reserve buys $1,000 of government securities from an insur-
ance company (or from any individual, for that matter), it
pays the insurance company with a $1,000 check drawn on

itself. When the insurance company deposits the check in its bank, a checking deposit of $1,000 is created for it, and the bank now has the Federal Reserve's check as an asset. This bank, in turn, presents the check for payment at its local Federal Reserve Bank and receives in exchange reserves equal to $1,000, the amount of the check. So far, the money supply has gone up by $1,000, and the bank has additional reserves. On the basis of these additional reserves, the banking system can now create *more* deposits by making new loans.

But what the central bank giveth, the central bank can taketh away. If the Federal Reserve *sells* government securities out of its portfolio, it *receives* a check for them, drawn on some bank; the Federal Reserve collects by reducing that bank's deposit at the Federal Reserve Bank, thus diminishing the bank's reserves. Result: both the money supply and bank reserves fall.

Note that the Federal Reserve could achieve the same ends —that is, change the money supply and bank reserves—by buying or selling any asset, such as record albums or any type of bond or stock. The reason for limiting its open market operations to the purchase and sale of government securities is quite obvious: who would determine whether the Federal Reserve should buy Bob Dylan or Barry Manilow? General Motors stock or IBM?

To summarize: these techniques—setting reserve requirements, varying the discount rate, and open market operations—put the reserves of the banking system (and their deposit potential) pretty tightly under the control of the Federal Reserve, thereby giving it sufficient leverage with which to control the money supply.

But does it really matter? What difference does it make whether the money supply increases or decreases?

Does Money Matter?

We have come full circle, back to the question that started us off: how much money should we have in the United States? What effects does monetary policy have on the economy?

Monetary policy consists of varying the amount of money in the economy, presumably increasing it (or, more realistically, increasing the rate at which it is growing) during a recession, to stimulate spending; and decreasing it (or increasing it at a less than normal rate) during a boom, to inhibit spending.

But whether just changing the money supply really can influence people's *spending* in any consistent way is not that obvious. Many appear to believe that monetary policy affects people's wealth and in that fashion influences their spending. Clearly, if people have more money and less of nothing else, they are wealthier and will probably spend more. But *pure* monetary policy—that is, monetary policy alone, without any accompanying fiscal policy (such as a budget deficit)—usually does not alter people's wealth *directly*.

An expansion in the money supply via pure monetary policy does not increase wealth directly, because the public gives up an asset or incurs a liability as part of the very process through which currency or checking deposits rise; the reverse occurs when deposits decline. For example, if the money supply is increased by Federal Reserve open market purchases of securities, the increased checking deposit acquired by the public is offset by the reduction in its holdings of government securities (they were purchased by the Federal Reserve). In any subsequent expansion of deposits by bank lending or security purchases, the public acquires an asset (checking deposits) but either creates a liability against itself in the form of a bank loan or sells to the bank an asset of equal value, such as a government bond.

What a change in the money supply *can* do directly is alter people's *liquidity*. Money, after all, is the most liquid of all assets. A liquid asset, as mentioned before, is something that can be turned into cash—that is, sold or "liquidated"— quickly, with no loss in dollar value. Money already *is* cash. You can't get more liquid than that!

Since monetary policy alters the liquidity of the public's portfolio of total assets—including, in that balance sheet, holdings of real as well as financial assets—it should thereby lead to portfolio readjustments that involve spending decisions. An increase in the money supply implies that the public is more liquid than formerly; a decrease in the money supply implies that the public is less liquid than before. If the public had formerly been satisfied with its holdings of money relative to the rest of its assets, a change in that money supply will presumably lead to readjustments throughout the rest of its portfolio.

In other words, these changes in liquidity should lead to more (or less) spending on either real assets (cars and television sets) or financial assets (stocks and bonds). If spending on real assets expands, demand for goods and services increases, and GNP is directly affected. If spending on financial assets goes up, the increased demand for stocks and bonds drives up securities prices. Higher securities prices mean lower interest rates. The fall in interest rates may induce more spending on housing and on plant and equipment (investment spending), thereby influencing GNP through that route.

At this point, it is worth noting that while monetary policy does not alter wealth directly, it does have an indirect wealth effect through its impact on interest rates and securities prices. Lower interest rates mean higher securities prices, and higher interest rates mean lower securities prices.* Capital losses are familiar to us all, and perhaps capital gains as well—even if only on paper. Such changes in the values of stocks and bonds in an individual's portfolio may very well alter his or her spending on real goods (a new home) or even on real bads (pornography). This indirect wealth effect provides another link between monetary policy and GNP.

Underlying the effectiveness of monetary policy, however, is still its initial impact on the liquidity of the public. But whether a change in the supply of liquidity actually does influence spending depends on what is happening to the demand for liquidity. If the supply of money is increased but the demand expands even more, the additional money will be held and not spent. "Easy" or "tight" money is not really a matter of increases or decreases in the money supply in an absolute sense, but rather increases or decreases relative to the demand for money. Indeed, changes in monetary policy are most often couched in terms of increases or decreases in the rate of growth of money, rather than in terms of absolute changes. In the past twenty years, we have had few periods in which the money supply actually decreased, yet we have had many periods of tight money because the *rate* of growth

---

*To avoid falling into the well-known Galbraithian footnote phobia ("No footnotes are sillier than footnotes"—John Kenneth Galbraith, *The Great Crash* [Boston: Houghton Mifflin, 1961], p. xxiii), we hereby offer our one and only:

Since it comes up again and again, it is worth devoting a moment to the *inverse* relationship between the *price* of an income-earning asset and its effective *rate of interest* (or yield). For example, a long-term bond that carries a fixed interest payment of $10 a year, and costs $100, yields an annual interest rate of 10 percent. However, if the price of the bond were to rise to $200, the current yield would drop to $10/200$ or 5 percent. And if the price of the security were to fall to $50, the current yield would rise to $10/50$ or 20 percent. Conclusion: a rise (or fall) in the price of a bond is reflected, in terms of sheer arithmetic, in an automatic change in the opposite direction in the effective yield. To say the price of bonds rose or the rate of interest fell are but two different ways of saying the same thing.

was so small that the demand for money rose faster than the supply.

If people always respond in a consistent manner to an increase in their liquidity (the proportion of money in their portfolio), the Federal Reserve will be able to gauge the impact on spending and GNP of a change in the money supply. But if people's spending reactions vary unpredictably when there is a change in the money supply, the central bank will never know whether it should alter the money supply a little or a lot (or even at all!) to bring about a specified change in spending.

The relationship between changes in the money supply and consequent changes in spending returns us once again to the speed with which money is spent, its rate of turnover or velocity, the subject of the following chapter. In subsequent chapters, we shall delve deeper into the influence of money and monetary policy on the economy—including interest rate effects, wealth effects, and maybe even a few special effects.

3

MONEY IN ACTION

When the Federal Reserve increases the money supply by $1 billion, how does it know how much of an effect this will have on people's spending and thereby on GNP? Say we are in a recession, with GNP $20 billion below prosperity levels. Can the Federal Reserve induce a $20 billion expansion in spending by increasing the money supply by $2 billion? Or will it take a $10 billion—or a $15 billion—increase in the money supply to do the job? As we noted at the end of the previous chapter, if people always respond in a consistent manner to an increase in their liquidity (the proportion of money in their portfolio), the Federal Reserve will be able to gauge the impact on GNP of a change in the money supply. But if people's spending reactions vary unpredictably when there is a change in the money supply, the central bank will never know whether it should alter the money supply a little or a lot to bring about a specified change in spending.

Clearly, this is the key puzzle the Federal Reserve must solve if it is to operate effectively. After all, the central bank is not in business to change the money supply just for the sake of changing the money supply. Money is only a means to an end, and the end is the total volume of spending (GNP); when the chips are down, GNP will determine whether the overall economy is performing well or poorly.

How stable is the public's propensity to spend on goods and services out of increased liquidity? Does the public react to a change in the money supply predictably enough to allow the central bank to calculate the effect of its actions on GNP? Or is the reaction so unpredictable that the Federal Reserve can do no more than probe and pray?

The Missing Link

When the money supply increases, the recipients of this additional liquidity probably spend some of it on financial assets, such as stocks and bonds, and some on real goods and services, such as cars and TVs. The increased spending leads directly or indirectly to a higher GNP. Moreover, the funds move from the original recipients to the sellers of the various assets and products. Now *they* have more money than before, and if they behave the same way as the others, they too are likely to spend some of it. GNP thus rises further—and at the same time the money moves on to a still different set of owners who, in turn, may also spend part of it, thereby increasing GNP again.

Over a period of time, say a year, a multiple increase in spending and GNP could thus flow from an initial increase in the stock of money. Whether this expansion in GNP is large or small, relative to the change in the money supply that set it going initially, depends on two things: first, on how much of the new money is respent on *real* goods and services at each stage; and second, on how quickly the respending takes place. If a large fraction of the increased money is respent by each recipient soon after receiving it, GNP will expand a great deal relative to the increase in the stock of money. On the other hand, if a small fraction (or none) of the increased money is respent, or if it is held a long time at each stage, or if many financial transactions intervene, the expansion in GNP during the year will be quite small relative to the enlarged money supply.

This relationship between the increase in GNP over a period of time and the change in the money supply that brought it about is important enough to have a name: the velocity of money. Technically speaking, it is found, after the process has ended, by dividing the increase in GNP by the increase in the money supply that started it all.

We similarly can compute the velocity of the *total* amount of money in the country by dividing total GNP (not just the increase in it) by the total money supply. This gives us the average number of times each dollar turns over to buy goods and services during the year. In 1982, for example, with a GNP of $3,060 billion and a money supply of $454 billion, the velocity of money was 3,060 divided by 454, or 6.74 per annum. Each dollar, on the average, was spent about 6¾ times in purchasing goods and services during 1982.

With this missing link—velocity—now in place, we can reformulate the problem of the Federal Reserve more succinctly. The Federal Reserve controls the supply of money. Its main job is to regulate the flow of spending. The flow of spending, however, depends not only on the supply of money but also on that supply's rate of turnover, or velocity, and this the Federal Reserve does *not* have under its thumb. Since any given supply of money might be spent faster or slower—that is, velocity might rise or fall—a rather wide range of potential spending could conceivably flow from any given stock of money.

The *ideal* situation for the central bank is a stable velocity, or at least one that is changing slowly and predictably over time. If velocity is stable or predictable, or close to it, the Federal Reserve can induce almost any volume of spending it wants simply by adjusting the money supply to the known velocity. For example, the velocity of the total money supply is now close to 7. If an *addition* to the money supply also turns over about 7 times a year in the purchase of goods and services, then the Federal Reserve knows for sure that if it increases the money supply by a billion dollars the end result will be an increase in GNP of about $7 billion. In that case, the Federal Reserve has it made; monetary policy alone would be both necessary *and sufficient* to control aggregate spending.

At the other extreme, the *worst* situation from the point of view of the monetary authorities is if velocity fluctuates randomly or perversely. If velocity moves randomly up and down without rhyme or reason, it would be impossible to gauge the impact on GNP that might result from a change in the money supply. If movements in velocity are perverse, that would mean that every time the Federal Reserve increased the money supply by 10 percent, velocity would respond by falling 10 percent. Monetary policy would be impotent. Changes in the money supply would merely be offset by an opposite change in velocity, leaving spending (and therefore GNP) unaltered. The public would not be responding to changes in liquidity and would be deciding by itself how much it would spend, irrespective of the actions of the Federal Reserve. Under such circumstances, monetary policy would be close to useless as a tool of national economic policy.

Living with Velocity

The facts are that velocity is neither perfectly stable nor fully predictable. Unfortunately for the Federal Reserve, it does not operate in a world designed for its own convenience. With a money supply of about $500 billion today, a miscalculation of only 0.1 in velocity means a $50 billion swing in GNP. But all is not necessarily lost. While velocity is not fixed, neither do its movements appear random or perverse. If the Federal Reserve could discover the underlying determinants of fluctuations in velocity, it might still be able to coexist with such a moving target.

With that in mind, examining the past may provide a clue to developments in the future. The velocity of the money supply (M1) reached an annual peak of slightly over 4 times per year in 1918. It fell slightly during most of the 1920s and then regained that peak of 4 in 1929. Thereafter, during the Depression and World War II, velocity fell almost continuously to an all-time low of 2 in 1946. In that year GNP was about $210 billion and the money supply $105 billion; each dollar, on the average, was being spent only twice.

Since then, however, velocity has risen considerably. It rose to 2.5 by 1950; to 3 by 1955; 3.5 in 1960; reached 4 (the previous peak) in 1964; continued on upward, beyond its previous peak, to 4.5 in 1968; hit 5 in 1973; 6 in 1978; and now, still climbing, it is approaching a turnover rate of 7 times per annum. The increase since World War II has been steady and even, with only slight dips now and then, usually in recessions, to interrupt an otherwise unbroken upward climb.

But, of course, facts alone do not speak for themselves. Understanding requires interpretation. Why has velocity behaved this way, especially in the past thirty-five years? After World War II it was generally expected that velocity would accelerate somewhat. Unexpected, however, has been the magnitude of the increase and its duration.

Perhaps the main reason for the extent of the postwar rise in velocity has been the increasing attractiveness of financial assets *other than money*—bonds, stocks, savings and loan shares, money market mutual funds, and savings accounts in commercial banks—as prudent and desirable outlets in which to invest excess cash. These assets are often highly liquid, almost as liquid as money, and yet they pay relatively high rates of interest. Attractive yields on financial assets other than money have led more and more people to wonder why they should ever hold any idle cash aside from what they need for day-to-day transactions purposes. And traditional concepts about how much cash on hand is really necessary for doing business have also come under reexamination. If cash for day-to-day transactions purposes can be pared down, then some of it can be loaned out to earn more interest. The money that is put to work moves to borrowers who can use it for current purchases. As a result, a larger volume of current spending flows from the same stock of money.

Corporate treasurers, in particular, have found that it pays dividends to scrutinize their cash holdings intensively. Could they manage to get along with somewhat less in the till than they had previously thought of as "normal," and invest a portion in high-yielding certificates of deposit at commercial banks or in U.S. Treasury bills (short-term government securities)? Increasingly, the answer has been yes, and imaginative new techniques of cash management have been developed to facilitate the process (also some not so imaginative old techniques, such as becoming "slow payers" when bills come due).

This trend has not escaped the attention of consumers. They have learned to economize on money by substituting lines of credit at retail stores and financial institutions in place of cash reserves; in addition, the growing use of credit cards has drastically reduced household needs for day-to-day transactions money. What was formerly held in the form of checking accounts or currency, for emergency use or for current payments, now shifts to higher interest-bearing savings deposits.

In summary, it is clear that velocity has not been stable; however, neither has it fluctuated randomly or perversely. There is a pattern in the movements of velocity during the postwar period—a persistent long-run rise with minor short-run dips during recessions. Even though we may not be able to pinpoint all the specific determinants, we can still see broad cause-and-effect relationships.

Higher interest rates lead to an increase in velocity by inducing business firms and households to economize on money. They hold less, lend out the excess, and others (the borrowers) can then spend it. Once learned, techniques of cash management are not easily forgotten, so that even in recessions, when interest rates fall, velocity does not drop back very far.

Furthermore, the long-run upward trend in velocity over the past quarter century suggests that fundamental structural relationships between the money supply and the spending habits of the community are apparently in the process of transition. New payment methods are developing (credit cards are a prime example), as financial innovation occurs side by side with technological innovation in industry. Such financial innovation, however, rarely takes root overnight. Established payment habits are likely to change only gradually.

Thus, although velocity is not fixed, neither is it likely to change drastically in the short run. The Federal Reserve may be able to live with it, even though it is a moving target. By gaining further insight into what makes velocity move, the central bank might be able to establish a range of probabilities as to where velocity is likely to be tomorrow and the day after, and act on that basis. In other words, a morning line on velocity (not unlike the one your local bookie puts out on the races at Hialeah)—provided the odds are unemotionally calculated and continuously reassessed in the light of emerging evidence—might still enable the Federal Reserve to come out a winner.

4

THE MONETARISTS VERSUS THE

KEYNESIANS

Each baby girl and tiny man
That's born into a family nest
Is either a little Keynesian
Or else a little Monetarest.

At an economics conference in the late 1960s, Robert Solow, a prominent Keynesian from MIT, commented as follows on a paper presented by Milton Friedman: "Another difference between Milton and myself is that everything reminds Milton of the money supply; well, everything reminds me of sex, but I try to keep it out of my papers."

Monetarists do, in fact, make so much of the money supply that they are rather easy to caricature. It appears frequently in their professional papers circulated among economists; it figures prominently in their policy recommendations to the government; and some have even shown how it can make money in the stock market. But so far, at least, no evidence has been presented on its qualifications as an aphrodisiac. Don't, however, rule out the possibility.

The president of the United States will use very different approaches in economic policy making depending on whether his orientation is Keynesian or Monetarist. As a Keynesian, he and the chairman of his Council of Economic

Advisers would spend considerable time pressing the Congress for countercyclical tax and expenditure legislation. If he were a Monetarist, he would expend more effort trying to convince everyone that things will get better by themselves; but if something simply must be done, then he would turn to the Federal Reserve. The Eisenhower and Reagan administrations usually followed a Monetarist course, while the orientation of economic policy under Kennedy and Johnson was primarily Keynesian. The Nixon, Ford, and Carter administrations used a little bit of everything.

What are the underlying differences between these two schools? And how do their theoretical disputes affect their policy recommendations?

The Monetarist View

The Monetarists used to be called Quantity Theorists. Their lineage can be traced at least as far back as Jean Bodin in the sixteenth century, through John Locke, David Hume, and then through the nineteenth century classical economists, David Ricardo and John Stuart Mill, up to Irving Fisher in the 1920s and 1930s, and now Milton Friedman in the 1970s and 1980s. Historically, they used to be concerned primarily with the relationship between the quantity of money and prices, viewing the money supply as the main determinant of the price level. The modern Quantity Theorists—or Monetarists—view the role of money in a much broader perspective; in the *short run* it is the crucial determinant of overall economic activity.

According to the Monetarists, there is a direct and reliable link between the money supply and GNP. That link is the predictability of monetary velocity. Because of it, a change in the money supply will change aggregate spending and GNP by a predictable amount.

The chain of transmission from the money supply to GNP can be visualized as working roughly in the following fashion. Assume that the Federal Reserve increases the money supply through open-market purchases of government securities. This increases the liquidity of the public; they are now holding cash in place of government securities. However, people do not want simply to hold this additional money. According to the Monetarists, people want money mainly as a medium of exchange for day-to-day transactions purposes, or to hold for a short while before making purchases. Based on the current volume of transactions—represented by the current GNP—they already had just about the amount of money they needed. So, finding themselves with some extra money, they proceed to spend it on real assets, on real goods and services, thereby driving up GNP.

If the money supply is increased during a recession, then the increased spending will primarily raise employment and real output; on the other hand, if the economy is already close to full employment, then the increase in GNP will consist mainly of higher prices. In either case, however, there is a close relationship between the money supply and nominal GNP (the level of economic activity valued at current prices).

How high will GNP go? The answer, according to a simple version of Monetarism, is that spending on goods and services will continue to climb until GNP has risen to the point where the relationship between it and the money supply becomes the same as it had been before the money supply was increased by the Federal Reserve. That relationship, of course, is exactly what we mean by monetary velocity (GNP/M). When GNP has reached the point where it once again stands in its previous ratio to the money supply, the public will finally be satisfied to hold the increased stock of money as a medium of exchange and spending will level off.

The same thing could be said in still another way. The increase in the money supply makes the public's portfolio of assets more liquid than it had been. This increased liquidity leads to the purchase of additional (less liquid) assets until the portfolio's liquidity is restored to its former state.

A decrease in the money supply works in similar fashion, except in the opposite direction. When the Federal Reserve reduces the money supply through open market sales of government securities, the public finds itself short of cash

"Frank, how ever did you find this guru?"

Drawing by D. Fradon; © 1968 *The New Yorker Magazine, Inc.*

relative to the volume of business being done. Spending on goods and services contracts, driving GNP lower until the previous relationship between GNP and the (now smaller) money supply is restored. Faced with a shortage of liquidity, the public cuts back its spending until GNP drops to the point where the original ratio of GNP to the money supply is reestablished and velocity falls back to "normal." GNP will then stabilize in line with the smaller money supply.

This particular view of the money-GNP relationship is quite inflexible. Most Monetarists would insist only that velocity be predictable, not necessarily a fixed and unchanging number—in other words, as money supply goes up, GNP rises by a predictable amount because the demand for money is related in a reliable way to GNP. Money demand might even depend on interest rates, but that relationship is predictable and stable as well. In either case, it is clear where the Monetarists got their name. The *ideal* situation for the central bank is a stable velocity, or at least one that is changing slowly and predictably over a period of time, and this is precisely *the* main assumption of the Monetarists. If velocity is stable (or predictable, as reasonable Monetarists argue), the Federal Reserve can induce almost any volume of spending it wants simply by adjusting the money supply to the known velocity.

In the Monetarist World, there is no need to even pay any attention to fiscal policy (the Keynesians' pet). Changes in the money supply can do the whole job, and stabilization policy should concentrate on that and that alone. No wonder Monetarists blame the Federal Reserve whenever *anything* goes wrong! Of course, there's still the question of whether we really need an active stabilization policy—a subject we'll discuss below.

The Keynesian View of Money

The gospel according to Saint John—the late John Maynard Keynes, that is—is that the channels through which the money supply affects GNP are rather different. They are less direct and also less reliable, primarily because velocity is not viewed as very stable or predictable in either the short or the long run.

The chain of transmission from the money supply to GNP can be visualized as follows. Assume once more that the Federal Reserve increases the money supply by open market purchases of government securities. Again, this increases the liquidity of the public. However, people *may* want simply to hold this additional liquidity. The entire process might end right there, before it has hardly begun. The public gets additional money and hoards it. Period. The money supply has increased but GNP is unaffected. Velocity has fallen. In the Keynesian World, unlike the Monetarist World, the public holds cash not only for day-to-day transactions purposes but *also* as idle balances or as a pool of liquidity for possible speculation in the stock and bond markets.

Suppose the Monetarists have a point: that people do *not* want to hold the additional cash. Finding themselves with more money, they proceed to spend it. In the Monetarist World they would spend it primarily on goods and services, thereby directly driving up GNP. In the Keynesian World, however, they would spend it on *financial* assets, such as stocks and bonds. The prices of securities rise and interest rates fall. The increased money supply may also increase the availability of credit as well as lower its cost. But GNP still has not been affected.

This drop in interest rates and increased availability of credit *may,* then, induce some business firms or consumers to borrow and purchase goods and services. *Finally,* GNP has been affected.

A decrease in the money supply works in similar fashion. The Federal Reserve reduces the money supply so that the public finds itself short of cash. The public may just hold less cash and that's the end of it. GNP will not be affected. Or, in an effort to get more cash, the public may try to sell some *financial* assets (or buy less than it had been buying), driving securities prices down and interest rates up. The higher rates, and accompanying decreased availability of credit, *may* lead to less borrowing and less spending, finally reducing GNP.

To summarize the Keynesian view: a change in the money supply can only affect aggregate spending and GNP if it *first* changes interest rates and/or the availability of credit, and *then* only if business or consumer spending is sensitive to those changes. In this way of looking at things, there's many a possible slip 'twixt the cup and the lip.

Is the Private Sector Inherently Stable?

A prominent issue currently dividing Monetarists and Keynesians is whether the private sector of the economy is inherently stable. Monetarists tend to believe that GNP will be relatively unaffected by autonomous shifts in investment spending. Keynesians argue that unless there is an active attempt at stabilization, the level of economic activity and unemployment will fluctuate considerably when buffeted by entrepreneurial animal spirits. While these beliefs have often taken on a religious fervor, they are grounded in the rather prosaic mechanisms of economic theory.

Monetarists, reflecting their classical ancestry, argue that any exogenous decrease in investment spending would be countered automatically by either increased consumption or other investment spending. The mechanism could be attributed, somewhat mysteriously, to the fixed money stock, hence a relatively fixed level of total spending based on the quantity theory. Or, to a reduction in interest rates that would follow a drop in exogenous investment. The fall in interest rates would, in turn, stimulate other categories of investment spending, reduce saving (thereby increasing consumption), and make up for the initial drop in investment.

As long as that mechanism worked, there would be no need to intervene by pushing policy buttons, either monetary or fiscal. The level of GNP would not be buffeted by exogenous shocks.

Keynesians are less impressed with the automatic offsets to gyrations in investment spending. First, the mysterious quantity theory linkage between money and nominal GNP is simply not part of the picture. Moreover, interest rates do not necessarily respond to a drop in investment. And even if interest rates did decline, there's no guarantee that they will induce very much investment. You can forget about any help from consumption—if anything, it makes matters worse by declining with falling GNP. Thus, according to Keynesians, it is essential for the government to step in and stabilize GNP.

Fluctuations in the price level are another source of stability, according to Monetarists. If, for example, consumption and investment don't rise fast enough to offset an initial decline in investment spending, the resulting unemployment will drive down prices. A fixed money stock with lower prices means a larger real supply of money (that is, in terms of its purchasing power over goods and services). This could stimulate spending directly via the quantity theory. Alternatively, the larger real supply of money would lower interest rates, and investment spending would increase still further. The Keynesian response to such price effects is twofold: first, prices rarely decline; and second, the spending effects are too slow to rely upon to restore full employment.

The Monetarist-Keynesian confrontation on the inherent stability of the economy at the full enployment level also has an important implication for the nature of the impact of the money supply on economic activity. In particular, if the Monetarists are right, then more money *always* means that GNP responds through higher prices rather than more real output. Even if the money supply were increased when the economy is in a recession, the forces restoring full employment (lower interest rates) would be already at work, so that the expansion in the money supply would produce only higher prices. Indeed, this is precisely the classical wisdom that serves as the Monetarist foundation. It also underlies the argument that inflation is everywhere and always a monetary phenomenon, as we will see in chapter 6. Thus, a key outcome of the inherent stability of the economy at full employment is that more money may mean more nominal GNP as predicted by the quantity theory, but the level of real economic activity would remain unchanged.

The Interest Rate: Where Does It Go and Why?

Returning to the monetary mechanism, it is obvious that, to
Keynesians, one of the keys to the effectiveness of monetary
policy is what happens to interest rates on financial instruments. Unless the increased liquidity produced by an expanding money supply lowers interest rates (and unless the
decreased liquidity produced by contracting the money supply raises interest rates), monetary policy is probably impotent.

Even the wealth effect of monetary policy, mentioned near
the end of chapter 2, which has been invoked by latter-day
Keynesians, operates through interest rates: Lower interest
rates imply higher securities prices, and higher interest rates
imply lower securities prices. Such changes in wealth may or
may not have a significant impact on spending. But if an
expansionary monetary policy is to carry with it a wealth
effect, it must lower interest rates; if contractionary monetary policy is to have a wealth effect, it must raise rates.

Monetarists, however, do not view interest rates as a major
link in the transmission belt between a change in the money
supply and the ultimate impact on spending. Indeed, in one
version of Monetarism, if interest rates do not change at all
it probably indicates a very *powerful* monetary policy, since
presumably the entire change in liquidity is spent *directly* on
goods and services and none at all in financial markets.

The controversy between Monetarists and Keynesians
over interest rates is even more complex. Milton Friedman
has argued that an *expansionary* monetary policy *raises* interest rates and a *contractionary* monetary policy *lowers* interest rates; just the reverse of standard Keynesian analysis.
How does Milton do it? Here's the point: An increase in the

money supply *may initially* lower interest rates, if the increased liquidity is spent on financial assets. But that is only the beginning. Once GNP responds to the increased money supply (as it must in the Monetarist world) the transactions demand for money will increase, thereby driving interest rates upward. But this is hardly new. Mainstream Keynesians certainly wouldn't disagree. The Monetarists argue, however, that the "income effect" of the increased money supply will overwhelm the initial "liquidity effect" so that interest rates snap back past original levels.

If pressed on this last point, Keynesians might even acquiesce as well: after a while rates *could* rise past the original equilibrium—it all depends on the speed and strength of the response in GNP to monetary expansion. They would focus their attention on the interim period—before GNP expands. And this interim period is sufficiently long to justify the statement: Expansionary monetary policy *means* lower interest rates while contractionary policy *means* higher rates.

But there's more. Until now we've ignored inflation. And while the complete Monetarist-Keynesian debate on inflation appears in chapter 6, it plays a key role in the response of interest rates to monetary policy. In particular, if expectations of inflation are generated by an expansionary monetary policy, then this will cause a *further* increase in the level of interest rates. The reason is as follows: A credit instrument promises to repay the principal of the loan after a certain time period plus an interest payment as a reward to the lender. The interest and principal are fixed in dollar terms. For example, a $1,000 one-year note which promises $50 in interest yields five percent. This is the nominal yield, that is, the yield measured in terms of dollars received. If the rate of increase in prices during the year is 2 percent, then it takes $1,020 at the end of the year to buy what $1,000 would have purchased a year earlier. Thus, in *real* terms the lender is receiving an interest return of only about 3 percent. It is simply a fact of life, therefore, that the nominal rate of interest minus the rate of inflation equals the real rate of interest. But if lenders expect prices to rise by 2 percent during the next twelve months and want to receive 5 percent in real terms, they will demand 7 percent from borrowers. As long as borrowers expect the same rate of inflation, they will go along with the higher nominal rate of interest. After all, if they were ready to pay 5 percent with no inflation, they should be equally eager to borrow money at 7 percent with 2 percent inflation—they will be paying off the loan in "cheaper" dollars.

What might lead *both* borrowers and lenders to expect inflation and then arrive at a higher nominal rate of interest? You guessed it—an expansionary monetary policy! When such inflationary expectations are tacked on to the income effect, Monetarists contend that it is virtually certain that these two will dominate the initial liquidity impact and expansionary monetary policy will lead to higher interest rates. An analogous argument can be made for contractionary monetary policy lowering interest rates.

Notice, by the way, that the Quantity Theory foundations of Monetarism are clearly visible in these arguments. Increases in money lead to inflation via the quantity theory. The interest rate is determined by savers and investors. They "pierce the veil" of money and refuse to let inflation interfere with their agreed-upon *real* rate of interest. Thus an "inflation premium" is added to the real rate and increases in money supply raise the nominal or stated rate of interest.

The story just told of interest rates rising due to the inflationary expectations generated by expansionary monetary policy has taken on an added dimension called rational expectations. In particular, inflationary expectations that incorporate the predictions of economic models, such as the quantity theory of money, as well as the predictable behavior of policy makers, are called rational expectations. They are rational in the sense that all potentially relevant information is brought to bear on the formulation of expectations. Nothing is left out.

The consequences of such apparently innocuous logic are simply amazing. In particular, if policy makers are expected to increase the money supply in an effort to lower interest rates, there will, in fact, be no effect at all on real interest rates since such anticipated money stock movements will have been already incorporated in portfolio decisions. For example, the liquidity effect of the anticipated increase in money stock will have already raised bond demand to take advantage of anticipated capital gains; thus no further bond price increases occur when the money stock actually increases. All that's left is the original quantity theory effect which says that increases in money stock raise prices. Thus, the anticipated rate of inflation generated by expansionary monetary policy pushes up nominal interest rates. There simply aren't any intermediate steps. Rational expectations provide a closer link between money and prices and between money growth and inflation and severs the usual Keynesian connection between money and interest rates.

While the rational expectations story sounds convincing, we must remember that the simple quantity theory operates only at or near full employment. At lower levels of economic activity, there is considerable slippage between money and prices. Even near what we designate as full employment there are wage and price rigidities because of contractual arrangements that interfere with any proportional relationship between money and prices.

Can we really be this far in a book on money and not be sure which way interest rates respond to monetary ease or stringency? Yes and no—unequivocally.

Monetarists and Keynesians generally agree that *initially* an expansionary policy lowers interest rates (and a contractionary policy raises them). But for how long? If the impact on spending is strong, or if expectations of price changes are generated, the initial interest rate change will be reversed and rates may very well snap back past what they had been originally. Thus interest rates could be either lower or higher at some point after an expansionary monetary policy, depending on the speed and strength of the response in GNP and on what happens to expectations regarding inflation. (Similarly, interest rates could be either higher or lower at some point after tight money begins, depending on the same factors.)

The question of the strength of monetary policy in affecting GNP will be explored in detail in the following chapter. It should be obvious, however, that the Monetarist view implies a very direct and certain impact of money supply on GNP. Money is only a temporary abode of purchasing power. Any increase in the money supply will soon be spent on goods and services. Thus Monetarists tend to believe that an expansionary monetary policy will be followed, rather shortly, by *higher* interest rates (and that a contractionary monetary policy will be followed by lower interest rates).

To Keynesians, the link between monetary policy and GNP is more tenuous. Changes in the money supply may or may not affect spending significantly. It depends partly on how much money the public wants to hold idle, and on the reaction of spending to changes in interest rates and credit availability. Most Keynesians—but by no means all—tend to believe that an expansionary monetary policy will be followed by *lower* interest rates for quite a while (and that a contractionary policy will be followed by higher rates for a considerable interval).

As an aside, we may note at this point that the Keynesians' skepticism regarding the efficacy of monetary policy is paralleled by their opposite stance on fiscal policy. Fiscal policy, you recall, is concerned with the manipulation of government expenditure and tax rates in order to influence economic activity. Keynesians believe that a change in government spending alters GNP directly; a change in tax rates alters consumer spending, also changing GNP. However, the Monetarists take issue with these alleged truths of Keynesian economics. We shall return to the details of fiscal policy and the arguments over its effectiveness in chapter 12.

Is It Money or Credit?

A subsidiary but important debate between the Monetarists and the Keynesians is whether the Federal Reserve, in conducting monetary policy, should look only at the money supply or at overall credit conditions as well.

The Keynesian analysis is a *credit,* as opposed to a strictly *monetary,* chain of causation. In a sense, money per se is seen as not too important until it finds its way into the hands of a potential spender. To a Monetarist, anyone holding money is a likely spender. But to a Keynesian, a loan transaction may be necessary to move money from its current owner, who may be holding it idle, to a borrower who wants to spend it. Thus the Keynesians take a credit view, concerned with financial assets, credit availability, the direction of interest rates, the reaction of lenders and borrowers to rate changes, and the role of financial markets as conduits for funds.

To a Monetarist, all this is excess baggage, more harmful than helpful. It is money that counts, money per se, and its effects on GNP are not roundabout but direct. To look at anything else is only a distraction.

As an illustration of a case where the two views diverge, assume that funds move from an individual to a business firm in a loan transaction (say the purchase of a newly issued corporate bond). The money supply remains the same; the corporation now has more but the individual has less. To a Monetarist, there will be no net change in spending since there has been no change in the money supply; the business firm, with more money, will increase its spending, but this will be offset by the lender, with less money, decreasing his. A Keynesian, on the other hand, would say that the result is more likely to be a net increase in spending; the lender is probably parting with what were idle balances, which in the till of the borrowing corporation will now be activated. The money supply is unchanged, but its velocity will increase.

The Federal Reserve has often followed a credit, rather than a strictly monetary, approach. Indeed, it frequently shies away from the term *monetary policy* in favor of the broader *monetary and credit policy.* Open market operations, reserve requirement changes, and discount rate movements affect credit conditions at least as much as they affect the money supply. Credit conditions include, among other things, interest rates on a wide variety of securities, the volume of activity in the various financial markets, bank reserve positions, credit extensions by commercial banks, and the flow of funds into and out of other financial institutions. The Federal Reserve considers all such credit conditions as well as the money supply when it decides what action it should or should not take.

A Compromise?

Monetarists claim that monetary policy should be conducted only for the purpose of controlling the money supply. Keynesians argue that interest rates and credit availability are at least as significant, maybe even more so. Monetarists contend that changes in the money supply are the major reason for fluctuations in GNP. Keynesians maintain that credit conditions are more important than the money supply, and, in any event, that fiscal policy is more important than either.

Ultimately, these differences can be settled only by empirical tests. As is often true in economic research, however, the factual evidence necessary to resolve the issues has been ambiguous at best and misleading at worst. There are credible (and incredible) empirical studies by eminent economists that come to diametrically opposite conclusions.

In its usual posture of deep humility, the Federal Reserve has refused to declare either interest rates or the money supply as the supreme channel through which monetary policy influences real economic activity. As the Federal Reserve sees it, concentrating solely on money market conditions and interest rates can lead to uncontrolled and even perverse movements in the money supply. Similarly, by focusing only on the money supply and related aggregates, interest rates are seen as subject to wider fluctuations than otherwise.

In a world of uncertainty, the Federal Reserve can never

be perfectly sure of the source of the decline in economic activity that it seeks to prevent, or the cause of the inflationary pressures it seeks to thwart. Under such circumstances, it feels obliged to focus on *both* monetary aggregates *and* interest rates in the formulation and execution of monetary policy. These points are sufficiently important to warrant further elaboration by way of some examples.

Assume that a decline in economic activity is on the horizon, precipitated by a reduction in business investment spending. The correct course to follow would be expansionary monetary policy: lower interest rates, increase the rate of growth in the monetary aggregates to pump liquidity into the economy, and thereby thwart the impending contraction with both barrels. If the Fed looked at interest rates as its only guideline, it would observe a fall in rates simply because business firms have decided to spend less and borrow less and because there is a diminished need for cash with a decline in economic activity. The Fed might simply do nothing, since interest rates are already falling—in which case the money supply would not increase at all.

Or, if the decline in economic activity is sufficiently great and interest rates fall by more than anticipated, policy makers may be induced to cut back on the money supply, thereby lessening the decline in rates but *lowering* the monetary aggregates. By requiring, under such circumstances, faster growth in the aggregates as a target of monetary policy, the Fed guards against such a perverse outcome.

Suppose, on the other hand, that the decline in economic activity is precipitated by an increased demand for liquidity by households—they want to hold a greater percentage of their portfolio in the form of cash. This would lead to less spending and lending by households, hence higher interest rates, and on both counts lower economic activity. The correct course to pursue is, once again, expansionary monetary policy to increase bank reserves and the money supply at a faster rate in order to provide for the increased demand for liquidity and to lower interest rates to encourage spending. If the Fed learned its lesson from the previous example and therefore concentrates only on the aggregates, it will expand the money supply. But if households' demand for liquidity is increasing at a faster rate, their spending will still decline, they will lend less, interest rates will continue to rise, and the contraction in economic activity will not be prevented. By requiring, under such circumstances, lower interest rates as a target of monetary policy, the Fed guards against such errors.

As long as there is uncertainty over the cause of fluctuations in economic activity, *both* interest rates and monetary aggregates must be used as targets of monetary policy. Monetarists place more emphasis on money supply and related aggregates, since they view velocity and the public's demand for liquidity as relatively stable and predictable. Keynesians rely more on interest rate targets, because they are less convinced of a stable demand for liquidity and a predictable velocity. The Federal Reserve—also known as the Great Compromiser—uses both.

PART II

The Power of the Purse

5

HOW EFFECTIVE IS MONETARY POLICY?

If monetary policy is to alter GNP, it cannot do it by mystic incantations. It has to do it by changing the consumer spending of households, the investment spending of business firms, or the expenditures of governments, either federal or state and local.

What categories of spending does monetary policy affect? To what extent? With what time lags? Complementing the theoretical discussion in the previous chapter and the velocity analysis of chapter 3, the purpose of this chapter is to present the state of knowledge in this area as precisely—that is, in terms of numbers—as possible.

Time Lags in Monetary Policy

By their own admission, Federal Reserve officials are not omniscient. If the economy starts to slip into a recession, it takes time before the experts realize what is happening so they can take steps to correct it. Similarly, if inflation begins to accelerate, it takes a while before the evidence verifies the fact.

Prompt recognition of what the economy is doing is not as easy as it sounds. For one thing, the available data are often inadequate and frequently mixed: new car orders will rise while retail department store sales are falling; farm prices may be dropping while employment in urban areas is rising. Furthermore, the economy rarely proceeds on a perfectly smooth course, either up or down. Every upsweep is interrupted from time to time by erratic dips; every decline into recession is punctuated irregularly by false signs of progress, which then evaporate. Is a change only a brief and temporary interruption of an already existing trend, or is it the start of a new trend in the opposite direction? No one is ever perfectly sure. This problem of getting an accurate "fix" on what is happening in the economy, or what is likely to happen in the near future, is called the *recognition lag* in monetary policy.

As soon as the recognition lag ends, the *impact lag* begins, spanning the time from when the central bank starts using one of its tools, say open market operations, until an effect is evident on the ultimate objective—aggregate spending in the economy. It may take weeks before interest rates change significantly after a monetary action has begun. Changes in credit availability and money supply also take time. And a further delay is probable before actual spending decisions are affected. Once monetary policy does start to influence spending, however, it will most likely continue to have an impact on GNP for quite a while.

Regarding the recognition lag, rough evidence suggests that the Federal Reserve generally starts to ease about half a year or more after a boom has already run its course, whereas it starts to tighten only about three months after the trough in a business cycle. This evidence is less than definitive, and it is likely that under some circumstances the monetary authorities will sense what is going on and take action more promptly than under other circumstances. Nevertheless, the inference that the central bank is typically more concerned with preventing inflation than with avoiding recession probably contains a grain of truth.

The impact lag is most conveniently discussed, along with the strength of monetary policy, in terms of the results that formal econometric models of the economy have produced. An econometric model is a mathematical-statistical representation that describes how the economy behaves. Such a model gives empirical content to theoretical propositions about how individuals and business firms, lenders and borrowers, savers and spenders, react to economic stimuli. After such relationships are formalized in a mathematical expression, data on past experience in the real world are used to estimate the precise behavioral pattern of each sector. A model, therefore, is based on real-world observations jelled into a formal pattern by the grace of statistical techniques. Thrown into a computer, the model simulates the economy in action and grinds out predictions based on the formal interactions the model embodies.

Our knowledge of how best to construct such a model is far from complete. The same data can produce different results depending on the theoretical propositions used to construct the model. As one cynic put it, "If one tortures the data long enough, it will confess."

A Keynesian model, for instance, would incorporate different behavioral assumptions than a Monetarist model and hence grind out an alternative set of predictions. Furthermore, the data we have available to feed in are not all that we would like. In any case, past relationships are not always reliable guides to future behavior; if they were, the favorite would always win the football game and marriages would never end in divorce.

Nevertheless, despite all their shortcomings, such models, if carefully and objectively constructed, are probably supe-

rior to casual off-the-cuff observations followed by inade-
quately supported generalizations. They are superior, that is,
provided they are always taken with a healthy dose of skepticism.

The Federal Reserve Board, together with economists at
the Massachusetts Institute of Technology and the University of Pennsylvania, has developed an econometric model of
the behavior of economic aggregates in the United States.
Many other economists have done similar work at other
universities and financial institutions. But our discussion will
be based primarily on the Federal Reserve–MIT–Penn
(FMP) model, called the Federal Reserve model for short,
which was prepared specifically to evaluate the impact of
stabilization policies on economic activity. The results of
Monetarist models, such as the one constructed at the Federal Reserve Bank of St. Louis, will be contrasted with the
Fed model.

The Impact of Monetary Policy on GNP

The latest edition of the Federal Reserve model—and there
have been numerous editions—includes virtually every conceivable linkage (maybe) between monetary policy and real
economic activity. Interest rate effects, wealth effects, and
credit availability are all explicitly articulated in mathematical splendor. As a first approximation to measuring the impact of monetary policy, let us look at what the model says
about the effect of changes in the money supply on spending
(i.e., on GNP). An increase in the money supply of $1 billion
produces an increase of $3 billion in GNP after one year, and

at the end of two years it is nearly $6 billion above its initial level. After three years, economic activity is still rising, producing an increase of more than $10 billion in GNP above its original level.

These results imply a rather long lag before the full effects of an increase in the money supply are felt on spending. If the Federal Reserve undertakes an expansionary monetary policy now, it will have to contend with the effects of such policies well into the future. This can create serious problems for monetary policy, as we shall see later.

Monetarists, especially those of the St. Louis variety, are unhappy with the Fed model. They don't like the detailed description of the transmission mechanism between money and economic activity, suspecting that the architects of the model may have unwittingly left out some of the *direct* links between money and spending. Exactly what these links are is not for us to know—but money works in mysterious ways, so we must have faith. The Federal Reserve Bank of St. Louis pits the midwestern virtue of simplicity against the sophisticated system produced by the Boston-Philadelphia-Washington Establishment.

The simple St. Louis model relating GNP directly to money produces a much faster and initially larger impact of money on economic activity. According to the St. Louis model, an increase of $1 billion in the money supply raises GNP by over $5 billion after one year, roughly double the impact derived from the Federal Reserve model over the same time intervals. After one year, however, the St. Louis model finds no additional impact of money on GNP.

Federal Reserve economists counter that the little black box connecting money and GNP in the St. Louis model does not lend itself to scientific evaluation. It is impossible to tell how much of the change in GNP is really due to changes in money supply and how much is due to other things that are changing at the same time. In short, the St. Louis model is too simple to be trusted by Easterners.

Some economists have argued that the effectiveness of monetary policy is asymmetrical—that is, monetary policy is more effective in stopping inflation than in getting us out of recession. They reason that the high interest rates and curtailed availability of credit that characterize tight money cannot help but force restrictions on spending, while the low interest rates and ample credit availability that are typical of easy money will not necessarily induce people to borrow and spend. You can lead a horse to water, as the saying goes, but you can't make him drink.

The Federal Reserve model provides some support for an asymmetrical response to tight versus easy money. In particular, a *decrease* of $1 billion in the money supply lowers GNP by $4 billion after one year and by $8 billion after two years. Thus the impact of tight money is more than one-third larger than the impact of easy money. The St. Louis model, however, makes no distinction between periods of easy or tight money. According to the Monetarists, money is money and if you want it and don't have it, it is equally as disturbing as when you have it and don't want it. (Yes, the sentence is written correctly; we checked it three times and so did the proofreaders.)

Returning to the question of time lags, it should be noted that it takes time for an open market operation by the Federal Reserve to have an impact on the money supply. Reserves provided through open market purchases, for example, must work their way through the banking system as banks make loans and buy securities. If we measure the lag in monetary policy from the point in time when the Federal Reserve injects reserves through open market operations, then we must add on a few months to the delayed response in GNP to monetary policy.

The Effect of Monetary Policy on Interest Rates

The impact of monetary policy on interest rates is also generated by our econometric models. Here again Monetarist models differ somewhat from the Keynesian variety. Most models show that interest rates decline and remain below their original levels for at least six months to a year after an expansionary monetary policy, and that they are above their original levels for a similar period after a contractionary monetary policy. The Fed model, for example, shows that a $1 billion increase in reserves via open market purchases by the Federal Reserve lowers the corporate bond rate by one-fourth of 1 percentage point initially; after some slight readjustment upward during the next twelve months, it levels off and remains below its original level for a considerable length of time.

The more sensitive three-month Treasury bill rate reacts with greater gyrations to an open market purchase. Immediately following a $1 billion purchase of government securities by the Federal Reserve, the bill rate declines by more than 1 percentage point. But after a year the bill rate is only one-half of 1 percentage point below its original level, and it eventually comes to rest about one-third of 1 percentage point below its starting point.

Under certain conditions, the Fed model does suggest that interest rates could rise above their original levels in response to an expansionary monetary policy: namely, when inflationary price expectations are especially strong. Even here, however, the decline in rates lasts at least through the second year of expansion. In contrast, there are some Monetarist models that show the Treasury bill rate snapping back to its original level and going above within six months after an expansionary monetary policy.

It should be emphasized that the response of inflationary expectations depends crucially on the initial state of the economy. At levels of economic activity that are very close to full employment, or when saver and investor concerns about inflation are especially strong, an upward jump in inflationary expectations due to expansionary monetary policy can be even quicker than was just indicated. Thus while the formal models show relatively slow adjustment, their predictions are based on the average historical experience. Any particular historical event can show more sensitivity than the average if the specific conditions are ripe.

At this point it seems useful to go one step further in examining the behavior of interest rates. Rising rates should cut off some spending and falling rates should be stimulative. Let us see which categories of spending are most sensitive to movements in interest rates. In this way we can isolate the specific channels through which monetary policy operates.

Investment Spending

One would expect interest rates and investment spending to move in opposite directions: an increase in interest rates, for example, should lower investment spending. If the cost of borrowing rises, business firms should presumably be less willing to incur new debt in order to build new factories or buy new equipment. The historical record shows, however, that interest rates and business investment almost always move in the *same* direction. As in most cases where fact contradicts economic theory, one of them must give ground —and it is usually fact.

In the historical record, many things are happening simultaneously, so that separate strands of cause and effect are not sorted out. Investment spending is influenced by a number of factors besides interest rates—by sales expectations, changes in anticipated profitability, pressures from competitors who may be installing new equipment, the degree of capacity currently being utilized, the availability of internal funds (undistributed profits and depreciation reserves), expectations regarding labor costs, and expectations regarding inflation, to name only some. An increase in interest rates may inhibit investment, and yet investment may, in fact, rise if a number of these other elements shift sufficiently to offset the effect of a rise in interest costs.

The actual change in investment spending from one year to the next reflects the net impact of *all* the variables influencing it, not just interest rates alone. We would expect, however, that if interest rates had not risen, investment would probably have expanded even further.

Econometric methods permit us to isolate specific factors, allowing us to experiment in the "laboratory" of statistical techniques, as it were. The effects of interest rates on investment, for example, can be examined holding all other influences constant. The results show that a rise in interest rates does reduce investment spending. In the Federal Reserve's model, for example, an increase of one percentage point (say, from 10 to 11 percent) in the corporate bond rate lowers business spending on new plant and equipment by about half a billion dollars after one year, by about $2.5 billion after two years, and by $4 billion after three years.

In this instance, the time lag is clearly quite substantial. In most cases, investment decisions are not made in the morning and executed in the afternoon. Decisions regarding the installation of new machinery and the construction of new plants are usually made many months in advance of their actual execution. Thus an increase in rates does not promptly affect investment spending. What it does affect is *decisions* currently being made about plans that will not actually be *implemented* until months or years in the future.

The Federal Reserve model does reveal, however, that there is one category of investment spending that is extremely sensitive to a change in interest rates. That category is residential construction, which, although it is not business investment, is still generally considered a form of investment because of the long time horizon involved, with returns accruing for many years into the future. An increase of one percentage point in the interest rate lowers housing expenditures by $3 billion within a year. In addition to this interest rate effect, residential construction is also affected by monetary policy through credit rationing by financial institutions engaged in mortgage lending.

Small business perhaps deserves special mention in any discussion of the impact of monetary policy on investment expenditures. Spokesmen for small business have always contended that during periods of tight money commercial banks discriminate against them in their allocation of scarce loanable funds.

The evidence on this is not altogether clear, but it is likely that small firms are indeed at a disadvantage relative to large borrowers during periods when banks are short of funds. Furthermore, large firms have access to the corporate bond market and other alternative sources of funds, while small firms do not.

On the other hand, the extension of trade credit (delayed payment for supplies) from large to small firms tends to offset some of these disadvantages. In effect, through their supplier-customer relationships, large firms pass their access to funds on to smaller firms in the form of trade credit. To some extent this alleviates the problem, although it is not likely that it eliminates it.

State and Local Government Spending and Consumer Spending

Construction expenditures by state and local governments also appear sensitive to the actions of the monetary authorities. Municipal bond flotations are often reduced, postponed, or completely canceled during periods of high and rising interest rates. Many municipal governments have self-imposed interest rate ceilings that eliminate them from the market when rates go up. In other instances, when interest costs become too heavy, local voters become reluctant to approve bond issues for school construction and other projects, since the higher interest burden implies the immediate or eventual imposition of higher property or sales taxes.

The Federal Reserve model indicates that a 1 percentage point rise in the interest rate cuts state and local government spending by almost $2 billion after six months. Subsequently, however, the impact declines as municipalities rethink their problems and, typically, proceed sooner or later with much of their planned expenditures.

Consumer spending, according to the Fed model, is influenced by monetary policy directly through the wealth effect of monetary actions on the values of stocks and bonds in household portfolios, and indirectly through the impact on the level of income. About one-third of the impact of monetary policy on GNP after one year occurs through changes in consumer spending, with another third coming from residential construction and the remainder divided between plant and equipment spending by businesses and spending by state and local governments. The effects on consumer spending continue to build up during the second and third years following a monetary action, while the impact on housing tends to stabilize as credit rationing by financial institutions becomes less important. After the first year, the thrust of monetary policy is reinforced by the delayed effects on business plant and equipment spending.

Lags Again

The evidence presented by both Monetarists and Keynesians suggests that monetary policy does have a significant impact on economic activity, with much of the impact distributed over two calendar years. There are powerful short-run effects but, at least as far as the Federal Reserve model is concerned, even more powerful long-run effects.

When the initial *recognition lag* is combined with the *impact lag,* however, the usefulness of monetary policy as a stabilization device becomes less obvious. Suppose a boom tops out in January but the Federal Reserve does not realize it is over until July, at which time monetary policy starts to ease. Its pre-July tightness may still be having depressing effects through the first half of the *following year,* but by then we might well be in the middle of a recession and in need of exactly the opposite medicine. The Federal Reserve, of course, will be providing that opposite medicine, but its expansionary effects may be so long delayed that they might not take hold until we are in another boom, thus once again making matters worse. Monetary policy will be a destabilizer rather than a stabilizer!

We shall return to the crucial topic of time lags later, when we discuss whether a robot should replace the Federal Reserve.

6

IS MONEY THE INFLATION CULPRIT?

Arthur F. Burns, former chairman of the Board of Governors of the Federal Reserve System, once told a visitor, "One of the greatest evils of inflation is that it leaves the President with no easy choices." When asked whether he thought the voters appreciate a real effort to stop inflation, he responded, "I like to think you are rewarded at the polls. But even if the reward isn't at the polls, I come from a culture where there is a belief in a reward in the hereafter."

Those of you who have been valiantly searching for the Eleventh Commandment can now rest easy; "Thou shalt fight inflation" has been added to the Scriptures!

To most of us, inflation is not something we pray for or against in houses of worship, but something we encounter in supermarkets, department stores, and, of course, doctors' offices. Needless to say, prices today are quite different even from what they were only ten years ago. Workers and businessmen whose incomes have risen along with the rising prices of the past decade can still visit their favorite stores and hospitals, although they probably can't stay as long as they used to in either place. But inflation is a more painful matter for many others, especially for the elderly and for retired or disabled people whose incomes are more or less fixed for the rest of their lives. At a sustained annual increase of 6 percent, prices will double every twelve years; at an

increase of 8 percent, they will double every nine years; and
if prices go up at the rate of 10 percent annually, they will
double every seven years.

Under such circumstances, it is obvious that retirement
incomes of a fixed dollar amount gradually melt away. A
retirement income that is initially adequate slowly becomes
marginal and, as the years continue to unfold, approaches
the level of sheer subsistence. About the only thing many
older people can hope for is that they reach the hereafter
before inflation does.

Who is responsible for inflation? Is money the culprit? Can
we bring an inflationary spiral to a halt if we clamp down on
the money supply? Can wage-price controls help?

Too Much Money Chasing Too Few Goods

The classic explanation of inflation is that "too much money
is chasing too few goods." The diagnosis implies the remedy;
stop creating so much money and inflation will disappear.

Such a diagnosis has indeed been accurate, painfully so,
during those hard-to-believe episodes in history when runa-
way hyperinflation skyrocketed prices out of sight and
plunged the value of money to practically zero. Example:
prices quadrupled in revolutionary America between 1775
and 1780, when the Continental Congress opened the printing presses and flooded the country with currency. The
phrase "not worth a continental" remains to this day. Germany after World War I was even more extreme; prices in
1923 were 34 billion times what they had been in 1921. In
Hungary after World War II it took 1.4 nonillion pengoes in

1946 to buy what one pengo could purchase a few years earlier (one nonillion equals 1,000,000,000,000,000,000,000,-000,000,000).

Pathological breakdowns of this sort are impossible unless they are fueled by continuous injections of new money in ever-increasing volume. In such cases, money is undoubtedly the inflation culprit, and the only way to stop the avalanche from gathering momentum is to slam a quick brake on the money creation machine.

Creeping Inflation

However, hyperinflation is not what we have been experiencing in this country in recent years. During World War II, consumer prices rose by about 30 percent. In the immediate postwar years (1945–49), after wage and price controls were removed, they climbed another 30 percent. None of this was unexpected or particularly unusual. Prices typically rise in wartime and immediately thereafter.

The unusual thing about prices and World War II is not that they rose so much during and immediately after it, but that they have never declined since. Quite the contrary—prices have continued onward and upward to this day, virtually without interruption, producing the longest period of continuous inflation in American history. In all prior wars, prices had gone up during and immediately after hostilities, but then had fallen back somewhat. Not this time. In all prior peacetimes, price increases had been interrupted from time to time by occasional corrective periods of stable or declining prices. No longer.

From 1950 through 1980, the cost of living increased in every year but one (1955). The annual rate of inflation over the entire thirty-year period averages out at close to 4 percent per year. Prices are now more than triple what they were in the late 1950s. They are more than double what they were in 1970.

This is not hyperinflation. It is not like America in 1775, Germany in 1923, or Hungary in 1946. This is a different sort of animal—nibbling away doggedly, insistently, without pause, at the purchasing power of the dollar. Prices do not skyrocket, they only creep—some years 6 percent, some years 10 percent—but always in the same direction, always up, up, up.

This type of inflation is something new. Is money the culprit here, too? Can creeping inflation, like hyperinflation, be stopped simply by slamming the brakes on the money supply? To work our way around these questions, it will be helpful to examine the recent inflation process a bit more closely.

Demand Pull

We understand fairly clearly—as well as anything is understood in economics, anyway—why the price level rises when aggregate demand exceeds the limits of the economy's full capacity output. This is the orthodox inflation setting, exemplified in starkest form in wartime when we simply cannot produce enough goods and services to satisfy all would-be purchasers at existing prices. The excessive spending (in relation to the available supply of goods and services) bids prices up, thereby eliminating some potential buyers and, in effect, rationing the available short supply among those able and willing to pay more.

War thus generates the classic form of demand-pull inflation, with competition among buyers for the available goods and services driving prices higher. People are put to work producing war goods—which are bought by the government —but the incomes they receive, unless siphoned off by higher taxes, are as available as ever for the purchase of private consumer goods and services. At the same time, the output of civilian goods is curtailed as war production takes precedence.

Part of the reason for our inability to eliminate the inching up of prices is simply that we have never really brought World War II to a complete end. An entire generation has grown up that has never fully known peace. Intermittently, in the past quarter century, the financial, manpower, and matériel resources of the nation have been mobilized in an effort to produce both guns *and* butter. Budget deficits, shortages, and accelerated consumer and business buying plans have periodically converged, with the swollen aggregate demand outpacing the economy's productive capacity.

Cost Push

But that cannot be the whole story. There have been periods of relative tranquillity, primarily in the late 1950s and early 1960s, and just after the Vietnam War ended, when international tensions eased and slack developed in the economy. But even then prices continued upward. For example, aggregate demand from government, business, and consumers was in no sense excessive during the years 1974 and 1975. If anything, demand was sluggish. Unemployment averaged about 7 percent of the civilian labor force during that two-year period. Nevertheless, consumer prices rose 12 percent in 1974 and 7 percent in 1975.

Why should prices rise when spending is slow and we are far below full employment of our labor force and full capacity utilization of our industrial plant? In past years, before World War II, these were the very times when prices *fell* and the impact of prior inflation was to some extent ameliorated. Some new ingredients have evidently entered the picture since the 1930s and drastically altered the economy's response mechanism.

One such ingredient is the economic strength of labor unions. The American Federation of Labor was founded in 1886, but the real power of trade unions to influence money-wages came with the passage of the Wagner Act and related legislation half a century later. On the basis of government encouragement of unionism as a declared principle of public policy, the expansion of the economy from the depression of the 1930s into the war boom of the 1940s carried with it an enormous growth in union membership. The ranks of organized labor jumped from 3 million members in 1933 to 9 million in 1940 and to 15 million in 1946. Today, union rolls list almost 25 million members. The Taft-Hartley Act of 1947 corrected some union abuses, but it put hardly a dent in their new-found power to extract wage increases in excess of productivity growth, thereby generating higher production costs.

A second new ingredient—closely related to the economic power of organized labor, although not so recent an arrival —is the substantial market power of big business. Because of the nature of modern technology, which often results in lower unit production costs as the scale of operations expands, a few large firms dominate many major manufacturing industries. Their size enables these industrial giants to exert a degree of control over their prices that would be impossible in a thoroughgoing competitive environment, thereby permitting them, to some extent, to pass on cost increases to their customers.

A third new ingredient is the Employment Act of 1946, under which the government assumed responsibility for maintaining high employment through the use of its monetary, fiscal, and related powers. According to the Employment Act, "it is the continuing policy and responsibility of the federal government to use all practicable means . . . to promote maximum employment, production, and purchasing power." Without the support of the Employment Act, neither Big Labor nor Big Business, individually or in concert, could sustain a wage-price spiral for very long. In the absence of the Employment Act, labor would have to take more seriously the possibility that it might be jacking up money-wages too far—that excessive wage demands might force businessmen to cut back on their hiring. Businessmen would similarly have to guard against pricing their products out of the market. But such restraints are relaxed by the presence of Big Government, standing ready to "insure prosperity" with injections of purchasing power should employment or sales decline too far.

Finally, in the past few years these three ingredients driving up prices have been joined by a fourth element: *imported* inflation. When the international oil cartel raised oil prices 400 percent late in 1973, we suddenly realized that our domestic price level has become extremely sensitive to actions quite beyond our control. Political extortion in the form of the 1973 Arab oil embargo had devastating economic impact. The prices that we have to pay for certain key imports from abroad—like oil and some other raw materials—have a pervasive influence on our own cost of living. When a well-organized international cartel, like the Organization of Petroleum Exporting Countries (OPEC), sets artificially high prices for its products and successfully limits its output to keep those prices up, the consequences include higher consumer prices in the United States (and elsewhere) regardless of the state of our domestic economy.

All of this has created an environment of inflationary expectations. And such expectations feed on themselves by forcing labor and business to enter contractual arrangements that pass on higher wages and prices in a never-ending spiral. The old-fashioned pattern of demand-pull inflation—excess aggregate spending, greater than the economy's productive capacity, pulling prices up—has not disappeared. But demand-pull (or buyers') inflation has been joined in the postwar period by a new form of inflation: cost-push (or sellers') inflation. Even when aggregate spending subsides, prices still rise. The distinguishing feature of cost-push or sellers' inflation is a rising price level while the economy is still below a full employment (full capacity) rate of production.

Money and Creeping Inflation

Unlike hyperinflation, money is not so obviously the culprit when it comes to the real problem of our times, creeping inflation. Take, for example, the five decades from 1930 to 1980:

"I've called the family together to announce that, because of inflation, I'm going to have to let two of you go."

Drawing by Joseph Farris; © 1974 *The New Yorker Magazine, Inc.*

1.   During the 1930s, the money supply (M1) increased by 35 percent, but consumer prices *fell* 20 percent.

2.   In the 1940s, the money supply increased by 200 percent, but prices rose by "only" 70 percent.

3.   The 1950s provide the best fit: The money supply and prices both rose by about 25 percent.

4.   In the 1960s the relationship deteriorated somewhat: the money supply increased by 45 percent, but prices by less than 30 percent.

5.   During the 1970s, however, the fit is somewhat closer: the money supply rose by 90 percent, while prices rose by 105 percent.

On balance, the data imply that money has a lot to do even

with creeping inflation. People will not be able to continue buying the same amount of goods and services at higher and higher prices unless the money supply increases. If the money supply today were no larger than it was in 1950 ($115 billion), prices would have stopped rising long ago—and so would real economic activity.

More specifically, an increase in the money supply is a *necessary* condition for the continuation of inflation, creeping or otherwise. But it is not a *sufficient* condition. Increases in the money supply will not raise prices if velocity falls (as in the 1930s). Even if velocity remains constant, an increase in the money supply will not raise prices if production expands. When we are in a depression, for example, the spending stimulated by an increase in the money supply is likely to raise output and employment rather than prices. Furthermore, in the short run at least, and sometimes the short run is a matter of several years, increased spending and inflation can be brought about by increases in velocity without any increase in the money supply.

Let us end this section with a summary statement of the role of money in the inflation process. Does more money *always* lead to inflation? No, but it can under certain circumstances, and if the increase is large enough it probably will. Case 1: If the central bank expands the money supply while we are in a recession, the increased spending it induces is likely to lead to more employment and a larger output of goods and services rather than to higher prices. Case 2: As we approach full employment and capacity output, increases in the money supply become more and more likely to generate rising prices. However, if this increase is only large enough to provide funds for the enlarged volume of transactions accompanying real economic growth, inflation still need not result. Case 3: Only when the money supply increases under conditions of high employment *and* exceeds the requirements of economic growth can it be held primarily responsible for kindling an inflationary spiral.

The time horizon and the extent of inflation are also relevant. In the short run, an increase in monetary velocity alone (generated by increased government or private spending), with a constant or even declining money supply, can finance a modest rate of inflation. The longer the time span, however, and the higher prices rise, the less likely that velocity can do the job by itself. Over the longer run, the money supply must expand for inflation to persist.

Conclusions: more money does not always lead to inflation (Cases 1 and 2), but sometimes it does (Case 3). In the short run, inflation can make some headway without any change in the money supply, but rising prices cannot proceed too far too long unless inflation is fueled by an expanding money supply.

Does More Inflation Cause Higher Interest Rates?

Unlike many of the questions we have discussed, there is relatively little controversy over the proposition that an increase in the rate of inflation leads to higher interest rates. This is true whether we go from no inflation at all to a rate of inflation of 5 percent, or whether the rate of inflation jumps from 5 percent to 10 percent. Irving Fisher, of Quantity Theory fame, was the first to recognize that inflation, or more precisely, expectations of inflation, would lead to higher interest rates on bonds. In particular, Fisher argued that the nominal interest rate on a bond was equal to a "real" rate plus the expected rate of inflation. A higher expected rate of inflation would lead to a higher nominal yield.

Recall our discussion in chapter 4, where the Monetarist-Keynesian debate over the response of interest rates to monetary policy was analyzed. Part of that discussion emphasized that a lender who is satisfied with a $1,000 one-year note which promises $50 in interest will demand a higher interest payment, say $70, if the price level is expected to increase by, say, 2 percent during the year. The reason: with 2 percent inflation, it takes $1,020 at the end of the year to buy what $1,000 would have bought a year earlier. Thus, when expected inflation rises from zero to 2 percent, the nominal yield on a bond must rise from (say) 5 percent to 7 percent to keep lenders happy.

Who cares if lenders aren't happy? Why not let them be unhappy, with the interest rate remaining at 5 percent? Under such conditions they might very well refuse to lend their funds because they would only receive 5 percent in nominal terms, which is reduced to 3 percent in real terms by inflation. If lenders refused to part with their funds, borrowers would be unable to borrow. And that would make *them* unhappy as well. So borrowers, realizing that they'll be repaying their loan with cheaper dollars, and to get their hands on funds with which they expect to make even more money, agree to raise the nominal interest rate on their promissory notes to lenders. That way everyone's happy, including Irving Fisher who said it all along: the nominal rate of interest rises by the expected rate of inflation.

Can we really be this far in our book and finally arrive at an issue on which everyone agrees? Don't be ridiculous! The story just told, of lenders and borrowers joyously arriving at a 2 percent increase in the nominal rate on bonds when expected inflation jumps by 2 percent, takes time to work itself out. In the short run, lenders might be induced to accept a lower real rate of interest. Thus, instead of the nominal rate of interest rising by 2 percent, it might rise by less, in which case the real rate would fall when expected inflation jumps by 2 percent. Eventually, as lenders adjust their cash balances and borrowers alter their investment plans, the real rate returns to its long-run level and the nominal rate rises above the real rate by the expected rate of inflation.

How long is the long run? Ah, if we only knew the answer to that question, how simple life would be. We get closer to Irving Fisher's result even in the short run—say within six months—as the delay in borrower and lender reactions gets shorter. Furthermore, when expectations of inflation respond quickly to economic forces, the Fisher result is likely to occur still more quickly. On the other hand, when delays are long and expectations of inflation respond slowly, then it takes longer for nominal rates to rise by the full amount of the expected inflation. As a general rule, it is a good bet that an increase in nominal rates of interest will closely follow a jump in inflationary expectations, but nominal interest rates are unlikely to respond immediately by the full amount suggested by Fisher.

The Trade-off Between Price Stability and Employment

Since inflation is not something we want any more of, and since the monetary tools to curb it are at hand, why don't we just use them and put a stop to these never-ending increases in the cost of living?

The reason we hesitate is because of an apparent conflict of national objectives. The cost of price stability—in terms of the unemployment necessary to get it—is too high. If we pursued monetary (and fiscal) policies with the determination necessary to put a total and complete brake on inflation, we would probably find ourselves with catastrophic rates of unemployment, at least in the short run. We do not want any more inflation, but we do not want any more depressions either. And so far we have been unable to find a solution to the problem of stopping rising prices without simultaneously bringing on at least a recession.

To put the problem succinctly, it seems that we cannot have both price stability and high employment at the same time. If we want stable prices, we have to sacrifice high employment. And if we want a high level of employment, we have to give up stable prices. Exactly what are the terms of this trade-off?

Chart 1 shows the rate of inflation and its associated rate of unemployment for every year from 1964 through 1982. In 1975, for example, we had 8½ percent unemployment and 7 percent inflation. In 1978, we had 6 percent unemployment but 9 percent inflation. Less unemployment but more inflation.

The freehand trend lines showing the relationship between unemployment and inflation are known as Phillips Curves, after their popularizer, Professor A. W. Phillips. The Phillips Curve for the 1960s indicates that to obtain absolute price stability then would have meant unemployment approaching 7 percent. In the early 1970s, absolute price stability would have meant unemployment closer to 9 percent. In the late 1970s and early 1980s, matters grew even worse.

Furthermore (and this the chart does not indicate), for many years the black unemployment rate has been approximately twice the national average. An overall national unemployment rate of 8 percent, which is about what it would have taken to eliminate inflation completely during the 1960s, implies a black unemployment rate at the deep depression level of 16 percent. Even worse, the black teen-age unemployment rate has been averaging *six or seven* times the overall jobless rate for many years; an overall national unemployment rate of 8 percent means a black teen-age unemployment rate of about 50 percent.

The optimum choice among this array of less-than-happy alternatives is not amenable to a purely economic solution. If we move to the left on the curve and choose low unemployment, some people will be hurt by the resulting inflation. On the other hand, if we move toward the right on the curve and choose something close to stable prices, other people will be hurt by the resulting unemployment. An economist, as an economist, has no basis on which to judge which is better. Resolution of this conflict of interests fundamentally involves personal value judgments and assessments of the social implications of the alternatives more than it involves economics.

Why has the Phillips Curve been shifting to the right since the 1960s, compounding our problems? One answer is that the trade-off between stable prices and high employment has gotten worse because of structural changes that have taken place in the economy. These include a changed composition of the labor force, an expansion in the demand for skilled labor but not for unskilled, more aggressive union behavior, increased market power in the hands of large corporations, and the international oil cartel.

But there is another possibility—no Phillips Curve at all. The trade-off between stable prices and high employment is

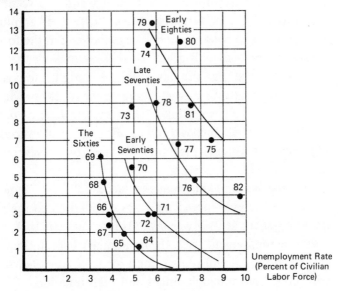

Prices and Employment: The Trade-off

illusory. That towering iconoclast, Milton Friedman, has pounced on yet another victim!

The Monetarist Challenge to the Phillips Curve

The Monetarist reasoning goes something like this: Government policies to increase employment generate rising prices; some additional employment can initially be bought with higher prices. But workers are not fools. They soon realize that rising prices are eroding the value of their pay raises. If they were satisfied with 3 percent pay raises when prices were stable, now they will want more to keep pace with inflation. If we assume 4 percent inflation has been generated, for example, workers will want 7 percent pay raises to get a 3 percent *real* wage increase. If employers believe they can pass on such a wage increase in the form of higher prices, they will grant it—thereby making the inflation worse. Then, as the day follows the night, unions will want even larger money-wage increases next year to wind up with another real wage hike. Thus expectations of further inflation snowball through round after round of ever-growing wage settlements promptly followed by corresponding price increases.

This has become known as the "accelerationist" hypothesis. It implies ever-increasing rates of inflation to maintain unemployment at its lower level. It also suggests that if and when unemployment rises, the inflationary expectations that caused the spiral will remain for a while, thereby leaving us with both high unemployment and high inflation.

On such grounds, Friedman argues that there is no true trade-off between employment and prices, because in the long run you can't fool all of the people very much of the time. You may be able to buy some additional employment with higher prices for a while, but as soon as workers catch on that their pay raises are more imaginary than real, either the inflation will accelerate or businessmen will begin to lay off workers. In either case, the Phillips Curve doesn't give the correct answer to the question of how high prices would rise if employment were increased by a given amount.

What should be done? Nothing, says Friedman. Let the economy find its own "natural" rate of unemployment. Don't try to lower unemployment by countercyclical monetary-fiscal policies, because they'll only produce inflation. It will only help for a short while, and the more you do it the worse things will get!

Is all this true? To some extent, yes. In the long run, the trade-off between employment and prices does get worse, as the chart indicates. But most of the evidence points to a rather long run—such as five years—before all the employment effects of increased inflation are wiped out. We can still use inflation to buy some employment—but less than we thought and for a shorter time period.

Wage-Price Controls and All That

There are other means that have been proposed to help resolve the inflation-unemployment quandary. These include manpower training programs, index-linked contracts throughout the economy, escalating annuities and social security payments, wage-price guidelines, and outright controls.

Manpower programs are aimed at shifting the dismal Phillips Curve to the left. There is substantial agreement that the fundamental cause of the present position of the Phillips Curve is the failure of labor markets to operate effectively. Less inflation would be associated with any given level of aggregate demand and employment if workers who are between jobs could be placed more quickly, if disadvantaged workers who make up the "hard core unemployed" could be retrained with skills that are in short supply, and if artificial barriers to entry were removed from certain trades and occupations. Manpower programs designed to rectify some or all of these structural maladjustments in the way our economy utilizes its labor force might very well permit us to coexist with an unfriendly Phillips Curve by pushing it to the left.

Since the basic problem with inflation is that it imposes costs—in the form of erosion of purchasing power—on certain segments of the public (widows living on pensions, and others whose income is more or less fixed in dollar terms), it is conceivable that one way to get around the problem of inflation is to compensate those who suffer most. This could be achieved by linking annuities and social security payments, and perhaps many other contracts as well, to some cost-of-living index. This has been billed as "living with inflation" by James Tobin of Yale and Leonard Ross of Columbia. Brazil has often been cited as a country that successfully used widespread indexation—that is, escalator or cost-of-living clauses—as a means of softening the impact of inflation. The main drawback of such arrangements is that they do not get at the heart of the problem, the root causes of inflation, and thus they may induce complacency about inflation and increase the likelihood of hyperinflation, where indexation always falls short.

Which brings us to wage-price controls. There are many types of wage-price policies—the strong variety, best approximated by wartime controls with stiff legal sanctions and rationing; the intermediate kind, such as voluntary wage and price guidelines with vague and largely unspecified penalties; and the weak variety, consisting of appeals to labor and business to act with restraint and integrity. Well, as the poet said, "Integrity ain't all it's cracked up to be"—so much for the effectiveness of the weak form of wage-price controls. As for the strong form of controls—few would argue, save perhaps John Kenneth Galbraith, that the benefits flowing from a full-blown set of wage-price controls would even remotely justify the bureaucratic costs and inefficiencies typically incurred in their implementation.

Wage-price controls once again involve trying to shift the Phillips Curve to the left. This time, however, we merely try to suppress some of the inflation associated with a given level of employment. But the costs cannot really be escaped. Inflation is inequitable—to those living on relatively fixed incomes. But so are wage-price controls—to those who were slow in joining the inflationary wage-price spiral before the controls were imposed. Even more serious is the interference of wage-price controls with the price mechanism that is so vital in channeling resources to where they are most desired in a decentralized unplanned economy. Indeed, even centrally planned economies appear to be moving toward *greater* reliance on decentralized price-profit signals to direct resources to their best uses.

Many European countries that have experimented with rather permanent wage-price controls (called "incomes policies" across the Atlantic) have concluded that they don't really work. Methods of getting around controls are developed as time passes, making them both ineffective and more inequitable. As an interim measure, however, temporary wage-price controls may have a greater justification and a better track record. If conditions are ripe for a slowdown in inflation, but inflationary expectations have become a way of life, imposition of controls may have some shock value.

Unfortunately, we cannot provide a happy ending to our story on inflation. The current state of the art does not have a solution to the confrontation of stable prices and full employment. Money is at the root of inflation in the long run but not the short run. The Phillips Curve is alive and well in the short run but not the long run. Wage-price controls work in the short run but not the long run. Living with inflation, as suggested by Tobin and Ross, may be a good idea —but for how long?

7

ARE HIGH INTEREST RATES

ALWAYS BAD?

It is time for a pop quiz. Compare yourself with the experts. Check all those you know, way down deep, are more true than false:

High interest rates

    ( ) result from collusion between Wall Street and Big Business.
    ( ) make the rich richer and the poor poorer.
    ( ) create economic disaster.
    ( ) raise prices and cause inflation.

We all think we know the answers. But do we? Have we ever really thought them through?

The Conspiratorial Interpretation of Interest Rates

There is a deep-seated suspicion in American society that conspiracy is everywhere afoot. Television programs are awful because "they" want them that way. Stocks go up or down because "insiders" are rigging the market. Rents are high because the landlords are ganging up on the rest of us.

The Yankees always won because that's how "they" wanted it; now "they" don't want it that way any more, so the Yankees win only some of the time. We've all seen too many Westerns. So why should interest rates be any different?

Insofar as interest rates are concerned—and regardless of the merits of these other matters—it is in fact extremely doubtful that any one person or group in the United States, aside from perhaps the Federal Reserve and the United States Treasury, has anywhere near enough power even to influence interest rates, much less set them.

That statement may be a slight exaggeration. But even if it is, it is still much closer to reality than the more popular conspiratorial theory of interest rate determination. The simple reason is that in this country there are too many lenders engaged in the business of lending, and therefore too many alternatives open to most would-be borrowers, to make it possible for any tightly knit clique of lenders (or borrowers, for that matter) to control the price of credit. They would love to. Who doubts that? But they are not *able* to.

Suppose that the three largest banks in the United States —the Bank of America, Citibank of New York, and Chase Manhattan—were to decide, in concert, to raise interest rates above prevailing levels during a time when there was *no overall upward pressure on rates.* Could they pull it off?

Not very likely. Quite aside from the antitrust laws, their business customers would simply shift to other banks, or decide to raise their funds in the commercial paper market (the market for short-term promissory notes of large corporations), or float bonds in the nationwide corporate bond market, or utilize any one of a wide variety of other potential alternatives. Consumers could also shift to another bank, or to a savings and loan association, or to their local credit union. If the three would-be monopolists wanted to continue doing very much business, they would have little choice but to bring their rates back into line.

Even the Federal Reserve does not have enough power to set interest rates at whatever level it pleases, whenever it wishes. The central bank may control the supply of credit, but it does not control the demand for credit, and both are involved in the determination of its price.

The facts of life, in this case at least, are rather prosaic. There is considerable competition in the market for loanable funds: competition among lenders for potential credit-worthy borrowers and competition among borrowers for the available supply of funds. Lenders charging more than prevailing rates will price themselves out of the market and lose business to their competitors. Borrowers trying to borrow at cheaper than prevailing rates will find themselves outbid for funds by others.

The Rich Get Richer and the Poor Get Poorer

Inequality in the distribution of income may possibly be getting worse. However, there is some hopeful evidence to the contrary in a few countries, including the United States, Great Britain, Scandinavia, and Castro's Cuba. But whatever the facts, the fault hardly lies with the interest rate, high or low.

The blame for continued bedrock poverty in the United States might conceivably be attributed to capitalism, but if so—and the evidence is less than convincing—it has little to do with the interest rate. Socialist and communist economies have interest rates just as capitalist ones. Indeed, regardless of the type of economic system, wherever funds are scarce and have alternative immediate as well as future uses there will be interest rates, whatever they are called.

It deserves mention, by the way, that financial institutions *pay out* interest as well as take it in. Currently the largest category of bank costs is interest paid out to depositors, a larger cost item than even wages and salaries. Assuming that all bankers are rich and all depositors poor, an unlikely assumption if there ever was one, the flow of interest on savings deposits—which increases when interest rates rise—redistributes income from the rich to the poor. The financial position of small depositors and bondholders is often ignored when the income-redistribution effects of high interest rates are discussed.

The fact of the matter is that the causes of poverty in this country have little to do with interest rates. The primary reasons for most of our poverty are much less complicated than the intricacies of money, financial markets, or fluctuations in interest rates. The poor get poorer because to a large extent they are elderly or unskilled or black or Puerto Rican or Mexican-American or Indian. They get poorer because they are elderly and inflation erodes their savings, or because they are unskilled and unable to compete in the job market, or because the skills they do possess have been made obsolete by the onrush of technology.

For many, poverty is quite simply the bitter legacy of several centuries of sharp-edged bigotry; the fruit of persistent, widespread, and systematic prejudice against racial, religious, and nationality minorities in education, housing, and employment. They get poorer not because interest rates are high but because they get third-rate educations in inferior schools, because they are denied access to clean and decent housing, because they encounter a mountainous avalanche of employer discrimination in job advancement and union discrimination in admission and apprentice requirements, because they are tangled up in a topsy-turvy welfare system that penalizes initiative, discourages family ties, and fosters dependency and cynicism.

For the most part, high interest rates are a contrived scapegoat. The elimination of hard-core poverty does not lie in perpetually low interest rates. It lies in an overhaul of our educational system, in adequate job-training programs, in more sensible welfare and social security arrangements, and in the maintenance of a high-employment economy without inflation within which there is full and complete equality of opportunity for everyone. (Will everyone please rise for a singing of our national anthem!)

Do High Interest Rates Create Economic Disaster?

Tight money and the high interest rates it typically induces are designed to prevent inflation or at least slow it down. However, some object strenuously to its use as an anti-inflationary weapon on the grounds that it is a very dangerous instrument that cannot be used in moderation—that if effective at all, it is likely to be *too effective,* setting off a financial crisis.

Thus, Alvin Hansen, for years the foremost American Keynesian, wrote in 1949:

The monetary weapon has the peculiar characteristic that it is scarcely at all effective unless the brakes are applied so vigorously as to precipitate a collapse. Those who glibly talk about controlling inflation by monetary policy have failed to consider that moderate monetary measures by themselves alone are relatively ineffective, while drastic measures may easily turn the economy into a tailspin.

A decade later, in 1959, in a report for the Joint Economic Committee of the Congress, practically the same thesis was reasserted by Warren Smith, who several years later was to become a member of President Johnson's Council of Economic Advisers: "It is perhaps just as well that monetary controls have not been very effective; if they had been, they might have been disastrous."

Ten years later, in 1969, the same views were put forth by others, particularly the labor unions, as soon as monetary policy began to tighten. And, as if such episodes were scheduled decennially, tight money during 1979 was again attacked by organized labor as courting potential disaster.

Assessments of monetary policy along these lines are paralyzing. If taken seriously, monetary policy would be employed so gingerly in fighting inflation that it could hardly be anything but useless. We have now had, in the postwar period, three decades of more-or-less active countercyclical monetary policy, sometimes devoted to offsetting recession and sometimes to counteracting inflation. And thus far, tight money, periodically imposed, has not precipitated either Hansen's tailspin or Smith's disaster.

Every economic policy involves some degree of risk. The Federal Reserve might indeed go too far. But on the basis of the record up to now, the potential depression risk involved in actively employing tight money to check inflation appears to be far less than the potential inflation risk of being afraid to ever use monetary policy at all.

In the years before World War II, mass unemployment was the dominant economic problem in this country. In the broad sweep of the postwar period, the major concern has not been depression, but inflation. We can't effectively fight the economic problems of the 1980s, if we continue to be hypnotized by the problems of the 1930s.

Do High Interest Rates Make Inflation Worse?

Although the announced purpose of tight money is to restrain inflation, complaints against its use have consistently come from critics who assert that the higher interest rates produced by tight money make inflation *worse* rather than better. Since interest is one of the costs of doing business, it is argued, higher interest rates, like higher wages, tend to *raise* rather than lower prices.

Long-time Congressman Wright Patman of Texas, who died in 1976 after forty-eight years in the House of Representatives, was a leading proponent of this point of view, along with spokesmen for organized labor. Surprisingly, there is possibly more truth in this position than most professional economists—who refuse to take it seriously and typically dismiss it out of hand—are willing to admit.

Higher interest rates *do* increase costs, and thereby push prices up from the supply side. They also *do* result in larger incomes for lenders, owners of savings deposits, and bondholders, enabling them to increase their spending and thereby helping pull up prices from the demand side. Cost-push and demand-pull. On the surface, at least, higher interest rates are not so different from higher wage rates. If the latter are inflationary, why not the former?

The standard response to these arguments is that interest

is so small an element of business costs, and of income, that higher rates don't matter that much. But such a response raises more questions than it answers. Indeed, it goes so far that it all but destroys the orthodox case for higher interest rates made by the proponents of monetary policy themselves —which is that higher rates lower investment spending, decrease aggregate demand, and thus reduce inflationary pressures. If interest is so minute an element of business costs, then how can higher rates be expected to significantly affect investment spending, as the proponents of monetary policy claim?

The fact is that interest is *not* a negligible item in business costs. In expenditures for long-lived plant or equipment, particularly, it may be a crucial component of costs. For example, if you buy a $50,000 house (it's very cheap, better check for termites) and get a mortgage for the full amount at 9 percent interest for thirty years, before all is over and done with you will be paying $93,000 in interest and the $50,000 house will wind up costing you $143,000. If the interest rate increases to 10 percent, your total interest payments will add up to $105,000 and the house will cost you $155,000, more than triple its list price.

Furthermore, interest is no trivial component of national income. In recent years it has been running at about 10 percent of personal after tax income.

The orthodox response, then, to the "higher interest rates raise prices" argument is wrong. If that were the only answer, the heretics would be far more correct than the traditionalists, even on the traditionalists' own grounds. The answer, if there is any, will have to be found elsewhere.

The answer to the "high interest rates raise prices" school of thought lies in a closer examination of the assumed similarity between the effects of higher wage rates and the effects of higher interest rates. In the previous chapter we pointed out that higher wage rates are inflationary. Wage increases in excess of productivity gains mean higher costs, thereby putting upward cost pressure on prices from the supply side. Higher wages also mean larger incomes for wage-earners, thereby generating an increase in consumer spending that pulls up prices from the demand side. Interest rates appear to do the same thing—and they do. Higher interest rates *do* raise costs and incomes, and *do* thereby generate cost-push and demand-pull inflationary pressures.

In the previous chapter we also pointed out, however, that wage increases, *alone,* could not fully explain either cost-push or demand-pull inflation. To maintain inflation for any sustained period of time, wage increases must be accompanied by continued injections of new money: permissive increases in the money supply are a necessary condition for the continuation of inflation. If the central bank does *not* increase the money supply, or actually reduces it, inflation will sooner or later peter out, regardless of the strength of unions or the monopoly power of business.

Similarly, high interest rates accompanied by monetary expansion are also inflationary. But rising interest rates attributable to tight money—monetary restriction—are not.

Rising interest rates that result from tight money should be equated *not* with higher wages plus an enlarged money supply, which is typically the equation that is implied, but with higher wage rates accompanied by a constant or lower money supply—as if every time wages increased by so many percent, the central bank automatically cut back the rate of growth in the money supply a similar percent. For this, in general terms, is what happens when interest rates rise during a period of *tight* money.

Such higher interest rates, like higher wages under similar

circumstances, may raise the price level briefly, but if the central bank sticks to its guns it will not go up far or for long. With a constant or lower money supply, further increases in the price level eventually would be difficult to finance. At that point the higher interest rates will choke off some spending and total expenditures will stop rising. Then the inflation process will grind to a halt (regardless of the higher costs) as a result of tight monetary policy.

PART III

Federal Reserve Policy Making

8

WHO'S IN CHARGE HERE?

Monetary policy is the responsibility of the Federal Reserve, but to whom is the Federal Reserve responsible?

The answer to that question is so complex that if we unravel it successfully (which is not too likely a prospect), we will either have unveiled one of the great socioeconomic creations in the annals of civilization, comparable to the invention of inside plumbing, or unmasked one of the most devious schemes ever contrived by the mind of man to camouflage the true locus of clandestine power.

According to some, the Federal Reserve is responsible to the Congress. But it is the president, not Congress, who appoints the seven members of the Board of Governors of the Federal Reserve System who occupy the stately building at 20th Street and Constitution Avenue, Washington, D.C. The president also selects from among those seven the chairman of the Board of Governors, the principal spokesman for the central bank.

On that basis, one might surmise that the Federal Reserve is responsible to the executive branch of government, in the person of the president and his (or her) administration. However, since each member serves a fourteen-year term, the current president can appoint only two of the seven-member Board of Governors, unless there are deaths or resignations. Even the chairman may be the appointee of the previous administration. Furthermore, it is Congress that created the Federal Reserve (not in its own image) in 1913, and it is Congress, not the president, that has the authority to alter its working mandate at any time. In 1935, for example, Congress chose to throw two administration representatives off the Board of Governors—namely, the secretary of the treasury and the comptroller of the currency, both of whom had been ex officio members—simply because they were representatives of the executive branch.

Others, more cynical, have suggested that the Federal Reserve is mostly responsible to the private banking community, primarily the 5,600 commercial banks that are member banks of the Federal Reserve System. The member banks do in fact choose the presidents of each of the twelve regional Federal Reserve banks, including the president of the most aristocratic of all, the Federal Reserve Bank of New York. It may or may not be significant that the annual salary of the president of the Federal Reserve Bank of New York is $145,-000, while that of the chairman of the Board of Governors in Washington is $69,800.

Who's in charge here? Who, indeed?

Formal Structure

The statutory organization of the Federal Reserve System is a case study in those currently popular concepts, decentralization and the blending of public and private authority. A deliberate attempt was made in the enabling congressional legislation (the 1913 Federal Reserve Act) to diffuse power over a broad base (geographically, between the private and public sectors, and even within the government) so that no one person, group, or sector, either inside or outside the government, could exert enough leverage to dominate the thrust of monetary policy.

As noted in the accompanying formal organizational diagram, the Board of Governors of the Federal Reserve System consists of seven members, appointed by the president with the advice and consent of the Senate. To prevent presidential board-packing, each member is appointed for a term of fourteen years, with one term expiring at the end of January in each even-numbered year. Furthermore, no two board members may come from the same Federal Reserve District. The chairman of the Board of Governors, chosen from among the seven by the president, serves a four-year term. However, his term is not concurrent with the presidential term, so an incoming president could find himself saddled with an already appointed chairman for part of his first term in office. The Board is independent of the congressional appropriations process and partially exempt from audit by the government's watchdog, the General Accounting Office, since its operating funds come from the earnings of the twelve regional Federal Reserve Banks.

The regional Federal Reserve Banks, one in each Federal Reserve District, are geographically dispersed throughout the nation—the Federal Reserve Bank of New York, the Federal Reserve Bank of Kansas City, the Federal Reserve Bank of San Francisco, and so on. Each Federal Reserve Bank is privately owned by the member banks in its district, the very commercial banks it is charged with supervising and regulating. Each member commercial bank is required to buy stock in its district Federal Reserve Bank equal to 6 percent of its own capital and surplus. Of this 6 percent, 3 percent must be paid in and 3 percent is subject to call by the

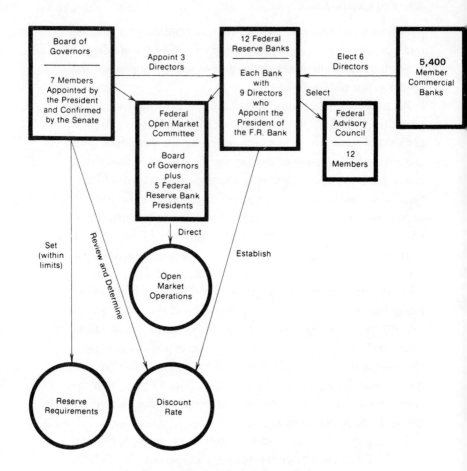

The Formal Structure and Policy Organization of the Federal Reserve System

Board of Governors. However, the profits accruing to ownership are limited by law to a 6 percent annual dividend on paid-in capital stock. The member bank stockholders elect six of the nine directors of their district Federal Reserve Bank, and the remaining three are appointed from Washington by the Board of Governors. These nine directors, in turn, choose the president of their Federal Reserve Bank, subject to the approval of the Board of Governors.

The directors of each Federal Reserve Bank also select a person, always a commercial banker, to serve on the Federal Advisory Council, a statutory body consisting of a member from each of the twelve Federal Reserve districts. The Federal Advisory Council consults quarterly with the Board of Governors in Washington and makes recommendations regarding the conduct of monetary policy.

Legal authority is similarly diffused with respect to the *execution* of monetary policy, as the diagram indicates. The Board of Governors has the power to set reserve requirements on commercial bank time and checking deposits, for example, but it cannot set them outside the bounds of the specific limits imposed by Congress.

Open market operations are directed by a body known as the Federal Open Market Committee (FOMC), composed of the seven-member Board of Governors plus five of the Reserve Bank presidents. Since the members of the Board of Governors are appointed by the White House, and the Reserve Bank presidents are appointed by the directors of each Federal Reserve Bank, who are (six of nine) elected by the member commercial banks, the diffusion of authority over open market operations spans the distance from the White House to the member bank on Main Street. In addition, although the FOMC directs open market operations, they are executed at the trading desk of the Federal Reserve Bank of New York by a person who appears to be simultaneously an employee of the FOMC and the Federal Reserve Bank of New York.

Legal authority over discount rates is even more confusing. Discount rates are "established" every two weeks by the directors of each regional Federal Reserve Bank, but they are subject to "review and determination" by the Board of Governors. The distinction between "establishing" discount rates and "determining" them is a fine line indeed, and it would not be surprising if confusion occasionally arose as to precisely where the final authority and responsibility lie.

The Realities of Power

So much for the Land of Oz. Actually, the facts of life are rather different, as the more realistic diagram, on p. 108, illustrates.

By all odds, the dominant figure in the formation and execution of monetary policy is the chairman of the Board of Governors of the Federal Reserve System, currently Paul A. Volcker. He is the most prominent member of the board itself, the most influential member of the FOMC, and generally recognized by both Congress and the public at large as *the* spokesman for the Federal Reserve System. Although the Federal Reserve Act appears to put all seven members of the Board of Governors on a more or less equal footing, over the past fifty years the strong personalities, outstanding abilities, and determined devotion to purpose of the chairmen—first Marriner S. Eccles, then William McChesney Martin, later Arthur F. Burns, and now Paul Volcker—have made them rather more equal than the others. As adviser to the president, negotiator with Congress, and final authority on appointments throughout the system, with influence over all aspects of monetary policy in his capacity as chairman of both the Board of Governors and the FOMC, the chairman for all practical purposes is the embodiment of the central bank in this country.

The other six members of the Board of Governors also exercise a substantial amount of authority, more so than is indicated in the formal paper structure of the system, because with the passage of time primary responsibility for monetary policy has become more centralized and concentrated in Washington. When the Federal Reserve Act was passed in 1913, it was thought that the Federal Reserve System would be mainly a passive service agency, supplying currency when needed, clearing checks, and providing a discount facility for the convenience of the private commercial member banks. At that time there was no conception of monetary policy as an active countercyclical force. Open market operations were unknown and reserve requirements were fixed by law, with no flexibility permitted. Since then, of course, the central bank has shifted from passive accommodation to active regulation, from the performance of regional service functions to the implementation of national economic policy. This shift has been accompanied, naturally enough, by a rise in the power of the centralized Board of Governors in Washington and a corresponding decline in the role of the regional Federal Reserve Banks and their "owners," the commercial banks.

It would not be unrealistic to describe the central bank today as headquartered in Washington, with twelve field offices located throughout the nation. These field offices may be known by the rather imposing name of Federal Re-

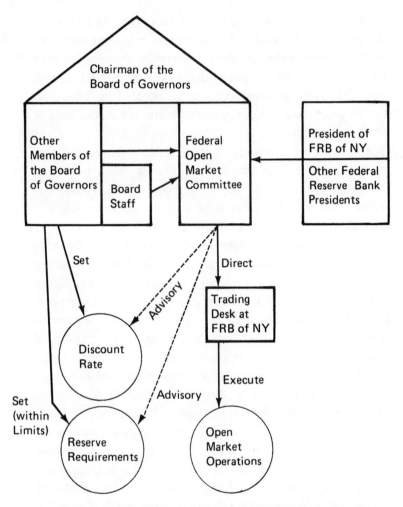

The Realities of Power within the Federal Reserve System

serve Banks, and they do indeed retain a certain degree of autonomy in expressing their views on the wisdom of various policies. But even so they essentially amount to little more than branches of the Washington headquarters.

Closely related to the Board of Governors in the informal power structure, and deriving influence through that association, is the Board's professional staff of economic experts and advisers. The long tenure in the Federal Reserve System of many senior staff economists, their familiarity with Federal Reserve history, and their expertise in monetary analysis give them a power base that is to a large extent founded on the respect with which they, as individuals, are held throughout the system. Through daily consultation with the individual governors and written and oral presentations before each meeting of the FOMC, staff personnel exert an indefinable but significant influence on the ultimate decision-making process. In fact, in recent years three members of the Board's staff (Robert Holland, Charles Partee, and Lyle Gramley) have been elevated to the Board itself, via presidential nomination. It is also worth noting, by the way, that in 1978 Nancy Teeters became the first woman member of the Board of Governors. The first black member of the Board was Andrew Brimmer, who was appointed in 1966.

Aside from the Board of Governors, its chairman and its staff, the only other body playing a major role in Federal Reserve policy making is the Federal Open Market Committee, which meets about every four weeks in Washington. Of the twelve members on the FOMC, a majority of seven are the Board of Governors themselves. The other five are Reserve Bank presidents. The president of the Federal Reserve Bank of New York is a permanent member of the

FOMC, and the other eleven Federal Reserve Bank presidents alternate the remaining four seats among themselves.

The statutory authority of the FOMC is confined to the direction of open market operations, but in recent years it has become the practice to bring all policy matters under review at FOMC meetings. Although only five of the Reserve Bank presidents are entitled to vote at any one time, typically all twelve attend every meeting and participate in the discussion. Thus, potential reserve-requirement and discount-rate changes are, in effect, decided upon within the FOMC, with the twelve Reserve Bank presidents participating in an advisory capacity. The Board of Governors, however, always has the final say on reserve requirements and discount rates if matters should come to a showdown, particularly since legal opinion appears to be that in case of disagreement the Board's power to "review and determine" discount rates overrides the authority of the individual Reserve Banks to "establish" them.

Once the Federal Open Market Committee decides on the appropriate open market policy, actual execution of the policy directive until the next meeting is the responsibility of the account manager at the Federal Reserve Bank of New York's trading desk. He is called the account manager because he manages the System Open Market Account, which includes all of the securities holdings of the Federal Reserve System. Since the FOMC's instructions are often couched in rather broad language, the account manager has to translate these instructions into actual daily purchases and sales of Treasury securities.

Like the account manager, the unique position of the president of the Federal Reserve Bank of New York in the hierarchy also stems from his role and status in the nation's financial center. If he is inclined to use this leverage, as Allan Sproul did a quarter century ago and Benjamin Strong before him, the president of the New York Reserve Bank can mount a substantial challenge even to the chairman of the Board of Governors. Since such a challenge would have little legal foundation, it would have to be based on the prestige of the presidency of the Federal Reserve Bank of New York and the forcefulness of the man who holds the position.

But where, in the corridors of power, does this leave the member banks, the directors of each Federal Reserve Bank, and the Federal Advisory Council? Pretty much shut out, if the truth be known.

The member banks do indeed "own" their district Federal Reserve Bank, but such stockholding is mostly symbolic and carries with it none of the usual attributes of ownership. The member banks also have a major voice in electing the directors of their Reserve Bank, but the directors in turn have responsibilities that are largely ceremonial. True, they appoint the members of the Federal Advisory Council, but the Federal Advisory Council serves mostly a public relations purpose and has little to do with actual policy making. The directors of each Federal Reserve Bank also choose the president of their Reserve Bank, subject to the approval of the Board of Governors. But the "subject to approval" clause has meant, in practice, that the most the directors can really do is submit a list of nominees for the position of president. On several occasions, the choice of the directors of a Federal Reserve Bank has not met with approval from Washington; such cases have made very clear exactly where ultimate authority is lodged.

How Independent the Central Bank?

The fact that ultimate authority over monetary policy resides in Washington brings to the fore the relationship between the central bank and the other branches of government also responsible for overall national economic policy—the Congress and the administration, the latter personified by the president.

The Federal Reserve is a creature of the Congress. The Constitution gives Congress the power "to coin money and regulate the value thereof." On this basis, in 1913 Congress created the Federal Reserve as the institution delegated to administer that responsibility on its behalf. Congress requires periodic accountability by the Federal Reserve and has the authority to amend the enabling legislation, the Federal Reserve Act, any time it sees fit.

Essentially, Congress has given the Federal Reserve a broad mandate to regulate the monetary system in the public interest and then has more or less stood aside and let the monetary authorities pursue this objective on their own and to the best of their abilities. Congress has also attempted to minimize interference on the part of the administration by giving each member of the Board of Governors a fourteen-year term, thereby sharply limiting any single president's influence over the board.

This semi-independent status of the central bank is a source of continuous friction. Some members of Congress believe that the Federal Reserve has carried its "independence" much too far. There has been some concern over its freedom from congressional appropriations and its partial exemption from standard government audit, as noted early in this chapter. Also, the Federal Reserve's responsibility on occasion for tight money and high interest rates has stimulated some intensive questioning at congressional hearings, including frequent scoldings of Federal Reserve officials by populist-minded congressmen who get uptight about tight money.

Others, in Congress and out, have complained that the Federal Reserve simply has not done a very good job, that we would all be better off if Congress laid down some guidelines or rules to limit the discretion available to the monetary authorities in conducting their business. We will discuss such proposals in chapter 11.

The relationship between the central bank and the president has also aroused considerable controversy. Many feel that the Federal Reserve should be a part of the executive branch of government, responsible to the president, on the grounds that monetary policy is an integral part of national economic policy. Monetary policy should therefore be coordinated at the highest level (that is, by the president), along with fiscal policy, as a component part of the administration's total program for economic growth and stability.

To do otherwise, it is charged, is both undemocratic and divisive. Undemocratic, because monetary policy is too important to be run by an elite group of experts insulated from the political process. Divisive, because monetary and fiscal policy should not work at cross-purposes. Since fiscal policy proposals are clearly within the president's domain, monetary policy should be as well. A Federal Reserve independent of presidential authority conflicts with the administration's responsibility to promulgate and coordinate an overall economic program.

On the other hand, the case for central bank independence from the president rests on the pragmatic grounds that subordination of the central bank to the executive branch of government invites excessive money creation and consequent inflation. The charge that an independent Federal Reserve is undemocratic is countered by the reminder that the central bank is still very much responsible to Congress, which can amend the Federal Reserve Act anytime it wishes. In addition, the president holds frequent meetings with the chairman of the Board of Governors, the secretary of the Treasury, and the chairman of the Council of Economic Advisers.

It is feared by many, and not without historical justification, that if the monetary authority is made the junior partner to the president or the Treasury (the fiscal authority), monetary stability will be sacrificed to the government's revenue needs—the government will be tempted to seek the easy way out in raising funds, by printing money or borrowing excessively at artificially low interest rates, in preference to the politically more difficult route of raising taxes or cutting back on government spending. The sole purpose of an independent monetary authority, in brief, is to forestall the natural propensity of governments to resort to inflation.

9

INDICATORS AND INSTRUMENTS

In the good old days, when government agencies told us only what was good for us, the Federal Reserve told us nothing. Does that mean the Fed was engaged in undercover activities —like bugging bank tellers? Quite the contrary, says the Fed. Always reluctant to antagonize the Wizards of Wall Street, the Fed simply wanted to make sure that the financial experts had something to keep themselves busy. And what could serve better than trying to figure out what the Fed was up to? If the Fed told everyone in plain English what kind of monetary policy was on stage and in the wings, what would the multitude of Fed watchers in the financial community do to occupy their time?

Actually, there never was anything cloak-and-dagger about the Federal Reserve. It has always poured forth an alarming volume of reports, pamphlets, magazines, monographs, and books that explained what central banking was all about. Guided tours and speakers were provided free of charge. Fed personnel were always delighted to discuss in detail why and how they did what they did—one, two, or ten years ago. But the *one* thing they were always reluctant to talk about—like central bankers throughout the world—was what they were doing at the moment and what they were planning to do next.

The Fed continues to behave as it always has so far as pamphlets, magazines, and monographs are concerned. But now, under congressional directive the Fed releases annual money supply targets for the coming year. Nevertheless, Fed watchers in banks and on Wall Street are busier than ever. Evidently what the Fed says and what it does are not necessarily the same thing! So join with us now in a thrilling adventure through the Federal Reserve Forest, as we search for that most elusive of animals: a reliable guide that will tell us what the Fed is really up to.

How Important Is the Discount Rate?

To judge by the press, many financial observers rely on movements in the discount rate to indicate the current stance and future course of monetary policy. A change in the discount rate is heralded on the front page of the *New York Times* and solemnly announced in respectful tones on the evening news. It is implied that when the Federal Reserve raises the discount rate, tight money is being ushered in, and when the discount rate is lowered, easy money is entering from the wings.

On the other hand, most Federal Reserve officials and academic economists agree that the discount rate is a follower rather than a leader of monetary policy. So what indicators should we study? In order to assess the importance or unimportance of the discount rate and other indicators of central bank actions and intentions, let us first examine discount policy in some detail and then compare it with the other major tools of monetary policy—open market operations and reserve requirements.

One of the primary functions of a central bank, perhaps

the primary function, has always been to stand ready at all times to provide liquidity to the economy in case of financial stress or crisis. As the ultimate source of liquidity, the central bank is responsible for promptly supplying money on those rare but crucial occasions when the economy threatens to break down for lack of funds. For this reason, the central bank has traditionally been called the "lender of last resort" in emergency situations. In more ordinary circumstances, it also lends funds to banks that are temporarily short of reserves. When the central bank lends, for whatever purpose, the rate of interest it charges is called the discount rate.

The discount rate was considered the main instrument of central banking throughout the nineteenth century and for the first three decades of the twentieth. It reached its apogee in prestige in 1931, when England's Macmillan Committee, somewhat carried away by the splendor of it all, reported that the discount rate "is an absolute necessity for the sound management of a monetary system, and is a most delicate and beautiful instrument for the purpose."

The long tradition behind discounting and the corollary importance of the discount rate stem from the fact that until the mid–1920s it was virtually the only means available to the central bank to accomplish its purposes. Now, of course, with other instruments also at the Federal Reserve's disposal, the relative role of discounting has declined noticeably.

It should be mentioned at the outset that discount policy has two dimensions: one is *price,* the discount rate, the rate of interest the Federal Reserve charges commercial banks when they borrow from the Fed; the other is Federal Reserve surveillance over the *amount* that each bank is borrowing. Thus, one obvious flaw in using the discount rate alone as an indicator of monetary policy is that the rate might remain unchanged while the Federal Reserve employs more stringent (or more lenient) surveillance procedures. Monetary policy could thereby become tighter or easier, even through discount policy, but without any change in the discount rate.

The objective of raising the discount rate is just what the Federal Reserve says it is: to discourage commercial banks from borrowing at the Federal Reserve. When banks borrow from the Federal Reserve, their reserves increase and on that foundation they can expand their loans and investments and thereby the money supply. Less borrowing at the Federal Reserve because of a higher discount rate thus means less bank lending to business, smaller growth in the money supply, and higher interest rates generally.

This process, it should be noted, provides no *direct* connection between changes in the discount rate and changes in market interest rates. The effects of a change in the discount rate are seen as operating through the mechanism of changes in bank reserves and the money supply, just as is the case with open market operations and changes in reserve requirements.

And yet, there does appear to be a connection between the discount rate and market interest rates. As can be seen in the following diagram, a close relationship often exists between the discount rate and interest rates on short-term money-market instruments, such as Treasury bills and Federal funds (the rate on overnight loans of reserves between banks).

The 1980 period covered in the diagram illustrates that there is no fixed relationship between the discount rate and other money market yields. Sometimes the discount rate is above the Treasury-bill yield and the Federal funds rate and sometimes it is below them. Moreover, careful examination reveals that changes in Treasury-bill yields and the Federal

Percent

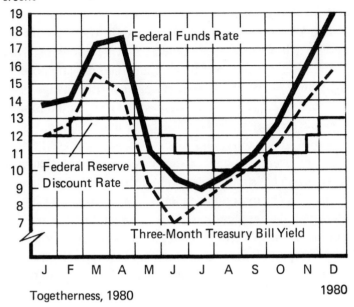

Togetherness, 1980

1980

funds rate typically *precede* changes in the discount rate. Treasury-bill yields rise, for example, because of Federal Reserve open market operations, and then—after they have risen quite a while and often quite a bit—the discount rate moves up. Or bill rates fall and then the discount rate is lowered. In other words, a change in the discount rate is likely to come *after* a basic switch in monetary policy has already occurred; it verifies the switch and reinforces it, but does not signal it.

One possible way that changes in the discount rate might directly affect market interest rates is through the "announcement effect" produced when a discount-rate change comes unexpectedly. An unanticipated rise in the discount rate is likely to lead bondholders to expect tight money and higher interest rates (lower bond prices). They sell bonds to avoid capital losses, thus hastening the drop in bond prices and the rise in interest rates.

The key, of course, is that the rise in the discount rate under such circumstances generates expectations regarding future interest rates. But if the public had already observed tightening in the credit markets prior to the change in the discount rate, the actual announcement itself would produce very little reaction. In fact, the bond markets might be relieved of uncertainty, and interest rates might even fall.

In any event, the bulk of the evidence suggests that while there may be some cause-and-effect connection between changes in the discount rate and changes in market interest rates, through expectations, for the most part the relationship is indirect—through changes in bank reserves and the money supply. It also bears repeating that typically a change in the discount rate comes after, not before, a basic shift in monetary policy. It confirms what is going on but does not anticipate it. As an indicator, therefore, it is comparable to a fighter who learns his opponent's right cross is on the way when it crashes into his nose.

Discount Rate Versus Reserve Requirements Versus Open Market Operations

If changes in the discount rate exert their main effects via bank reserves and the money supply, it is relevant to compare them in this respect with the other tools of monetary policy—changes in reserve requirements and open market operations.

During the 1950s, 1960s and 1970s, borrowings from the

Federal Reserve averaged about half a billion dollars annually. Even at its occasional peak levels, discounting never provided more than 10 percent of total bank reserves and usually the percentage was much less—on average about 2 or 3 percent. Moreover, a change in the discount rate affects only those banks that are in debt to the Federal Reserve, or that consider such borrowing to be a likely source of funds. Many banks never borrow from the Federal Reserve except in dire emergency.

Reserve-requirement changes, on the other hand, have an extremely powerful impact on bank-reserve positions and the money supply. A small change in the required reserve ratio instantly produces a rather large change in bank excess reserves. Because the impact is so powerful, so blunt, so immediate, and so widespread, the Federal Reserve uses its authority to change reserve requirements only sparingly, particularly during tight money periods when increases in reserve requirements would be appropriate.

After all is said and done, the day-by-day standby of monetary policy, in good times and bad, is open market operations. The purchase or sale of government securities can be undertaken in large or small amounts, as the Federal Reserve chooses. The impact is fairly prompt; it is possible to proceed gradually and to reverse field rapidly.

One reason market interest rates change before the discount rate changes is precisely because the Federal Reserve has already been active with open market operations. When the Federal Reserve alters the direction of monetary policy, it is open market operations that typically lead the way. It is also open market operations that do the brunt of the work as the new policy gathers momentum, with back-up support where necessary and appropriate from the discount rate and reserve requirements.

A Pride of Lions, a Gaggle of Geese, and a Plethora of Indicators

Unfortunately, since open market operations are so unobtrusive, the search for reliable indicators of what the central bank is up to becomes more difficult than ever. The discount rate is generally not too helpful a guide to what the Federal Reserve is doing, except as confirmation of a change in monetary policy that has already occurred. A change in the direction of monetary policy can occur without any change in the discount rate, and conversely a change in the discount rate does not normally initiate a change in Federal Reserve policy.

Reserve requirement changes are not of much assistance because they are used so seldom. Paradoxically, open market operations are not very helpful for the opposite reason—they are used too frequently.

Weekly data on Federal Reserve open market operations are released every Friday afternoon and published in Saturday's papers. But the knowledge that the Federal Reserve bought or sold so many government securities during any one week, or even over a succession of weeks, is in itself of limited value; the transactions may have been made simply to offset some "outside" factors that were affecting bank reserves, such as a seasonal inflow of currency, changes in the Treasury's cash balances, or any of a multitude of other possibilities.

Since it is widely understood that weekly data on open market operations alone give an inadequate picture of what is going on, many financial observers rely more on movements in interest rates for clues to the current stance of monetary policy. Of all yields, the ones most quickly responsive to monetary policy are probably the rate on short-term Treasury bills and the Federal funds rate. The Federal funds rate is the rate charged on reserves lent from one bank to another. On any given day, some banks have excess reserves and other banks have reserve deficiencies. There are brokers who bring such banks together to arrange for a loan (called a purchase and sale) from banks with surplus reserves to banks with deficient reserves. The agreed upon interest rate is called the Federal funds rate. It can rise significantly when there are few banks with excess reserves and lots with reserve deficiencies, and it can drop just as precipitously when the reserve rich banks outnumber the poor. Thus it acts as a sensitive barometer of conditions in the reserves market.

However, as reliable indicators of what the central bank is doing, all interest rates have serious limitations. To Monetarists, of course, as we saw in chapter 4, they are irrelevant. Aside from that, it should be obvious that they are susceptible to change for reasons other than Federal Reserve policy; this makes it dangerous to read them as though they were determined exclusively by the Federal Reserve. The central bank has a substantial influence over the supply of credit, but only limited influence over the demand for it, so that interest rates may fluctuate for reasons that have nothing to do with the Federal Reserve's actions. Tight money generally means a rise in interest rates, but a rise in interest rates does not necessarily mean tight money. Indeed, as we saw in chapter 4, excessively *easy* money might also produce a rise in interest rates.

Given the shortcomings of all the "orthodox" indicators —the discount rate, open market transactions, and the behavior of interest rates—the Federal Reserve, always helpful, releases a truckload of numbers each Friday afternoon along with the data on open market operations. It presents current statistics on a wide variety of alternative indicators. You can take your pick!

It lists weekly figures on all of the following: the monetary base, total member-bank reserves, the volume of member-bank discounting from the Federal Reserve, free reserves, various measures of the money supply, business loans at large commercial banks, and a few hundred other numbers just for good measure.

All these are self-explanatory except perhaps the monetary base and free reserves. The monetary base is defined as total member-bank reserves plus currency outstanding. Free reserves equals member-bank excess reserves less their borrowings from the Federal Reserve; when borrowings exceed excess reserves, it is usually called net borrowed reserves.

With this smorgasbord of indicators, plus the orthodox ones that are on the back burner, you can select those that best suit your individual taste. As is obvious from chapter 4, a Monetarist will lean toward the money supply in one form or another, a Keynesian toward interest rates and business loans. An eclectic will stuff himself on a little bit of everything, and if life becomes more complicated that way he has only himself to blame.

Free reserves attained some degree of popularity a few years ago but have fallen from favor. The main trouble is that a given level of free reserves is compatible with many different levels of the money supply and bank credit. The figure for free reserves has fluctuated within roughly the same limits for the past twenty years, while the money supply and bank credit have grown considerably during that interval.

At the same time as the Monetarists are downgrading interest rates as indicators of Federal Reserve policy, because they are not under the firm control of the central bank, Keynesians are saying the same thing about the money supply—that it is influenced by commercial bank behavior in conjunction with swings in economic activity, and that it can be controlled only imperfectly by the Federal Reserve. For example, as interest rates on bank loans and investments rise (relative to the discount rate) during a business upswing, banks borrow more from the discount window, expand their loans, and increase the money supply. Similarly, as interest rates fall, perhaps because of a slowdown in economic activity, banks repay their borrowings at the Federal Reserve, reduce their loans, and contract the money supply. If it is the central bank that is solely responsible for changes in the money supply, then it is a good indicator of Federal Reserve policy. But if the money supply can change regardless of Federal Reserve intentions, then using it as an indicator is likely to throw you off the track.

In order to save the money supply as an indicator of monetary policy, Monetarists have marshaled statistical evidence showing that it is Federal Reserve initiative—open market operations and reserve-requirement changes—that is the main cause of movements in the money supply. As a backup, however, they propose the monetary base as an alternative indicator, a first cousin to the money supply but somewhat more directly under the Federal Reserve's thumb.

Other Federal Reservologists prefer total reserves to the monetary base. For still others, including the architects of the Federal Reserve–MIT–Penn model, total reserves must be purged of reserves arising from member bank borrowing at the discount window—leaving us with nonborrowed reserves to chart the course. In point of fact, between October 1979 and August 1982, when the Fed took aim at controlling the money supply, nonborrowed reserves was the best signal to follow.

By this time, things have clearly gotten out of hand as far

as the Monetarists are concerned, and they disassociate themselves from anything further removed from the money supply than the monetary base.

Confused? Read on.

Some Helpful Hints

Where does all this leave someone who is trying to make an honest buck evaluating the posture of monetary policy? Instead of responding with a cliché (as is our custom)—such as "Life is tough for everyone"—we offer a series of helpful hints (HHs) to aid in interpreting Federal Reserve behavior.

1.   Divide the indicators into two groups. One: *the monetary and reserve aggregates*—including the money supply (your favorite flavor), the monetary base, and reserves. Two: *money market conditions*—especially interest rates on Treasury bills and the Federal funds rate.

2.   Do not conclude that, because there has been an increase in the aggregates, monetary policy is embarked on a wild expansion. The money supply, for example, must increase with a growing economy in order to provide funds for the increased transactions associated with a larger GNP. The money supply has, in fact, increased in every year since 1950, although it can and has declined over shorter intervals (say three or six months).

3.   Try to judge whether the aggregates, say the money supply, are growing faster than normal (expansionary policy) or slower than normal (restrictive policy). What is normal?

The money supply grew at an annual rate of 4.0 percent during the twenty years from 1955 through 1975. From 1955 through 1965, however, its growth was only 2.2 percent a year, from 1966 through 1975 it was 5.9 percent, and from 1975 through 1982 the growth rate was 7.0 percent. Take your pick.

4.   If interest rates are falling at the same time as the aggregates are increasing at a faster-than-normal rate, it is a good bet that the Federal Reserve has embarked on a course of monetary expansion. And if interest rates are rising at the same time as the aggregates are growing at a slower-than-normal rate, it is an equally good bet that the Federal Reserve has begun to exercise restraint.

5.   The Federal Reserve publishes the minutes of the FOMC meetings with a thirty-day delay. Read them. If the Federal Reserve decided on increased monetary ease a month ago and your reading of the indicators shows it has not succeeded, look for signs of further easing as the Fed tries harder. If tighter monetary policy was decided upon a month ago and your reading of the indicators shows that the Federal Reserve hasn't succeeded—call your broker and sell (see chapter 14 first).

Naturally, we assume no responsibility for the misfortunes brought down upon you when following these HHs. But we insist on 10 percent of the profits. For those of you who prefer to construct your own "super indicator" for monetary policy, you are invited to read the next chapter, which explains how to read the directive issued at the FOMC meetings and also treats you to a detailed look at the mechanics of open market operations.

10

THE NUTS AND BOLTS OF

MONETARY POLICY

At 11:15 in the morning of each business day, a long-distance conference call takes place among three men: Peter Sternlight, the manager of the System Open Market Account, who is located in the Federal Reserve Bank of New York; a member of the Board of Governors in Washington, D.C.; and a president of one of the other Federal Reserve banks currently serving on the Federal Open Market Committee. The job of the account manager is to carry out open market operations for the purpose of implementing the monetary policy directive issued at the last meeting of the FOMC. Each morning he reviews the operations planned for the day via the telephone hookup.

Although we have never listened in to what is said during one of these calls, we can make a pretty good guess at the conversation, much as sports commentators are able to surmise what is said at those all-important conferences between the quarterback and his coach in the closing minutes of a game, or the even more important huddle between a pitcher and catcher with men on second and third and none out. It probably goes something like this:

OPERATOR: San Francisco and Washington are standing by, New York. Will you deposit $3.35, please?

NEW YORK: You mean it's our turn to pay? Hold on a minute, operator, we don't seem to have enough change here.

WASHINGTON: This is Chairman Volcker on the line.

NEW YORK: Sorry, there's no one here by that name.

WASHINGTON: No, you don't seem to understand, I'm Chairman Paul Volcker and I want . . .

NEW YORK: Hello Paul, it's Peter. Sorry for the mix-up, but we've just hired a few Ph.Ds to man the phones, and they haven't gotten the hang of it quite yet.

WASHINGTON: I know just what you mean. Say, we've got a problem here. Our staff says the 6½ to 9 percent range for M1 should replace as the main target the 4 to 6½ percent range on M2. Or is it the other way around?

NEW YORK: Frankly, our people have urged me to look at the M3 numbers, trying to hit the fourth-quarter-to-fourth-quarter growth figures, rather than the two-month targets. They say the M1 ball game is over.

SAN FRANCISCO: Hello? Hello? When do we start?

If you think we have exaggerated the potential confusion confronting the account manager, a reading of some of the FOMC operating instructions should convince you otherwise. The primary thrust of monetary policy is summarized in the FOMC directive. Let's take a detailed look at how it is formulated and the ways in which it can be interpreted. We can then turn to the open market operations used in carrying it out.

The FOMC Directive

The Federal Open Market Committee meets about once every four weeks. At the beginning of each meeting, the staff of the FOMC, comprised of economists from the Board of Governors and the district Federal Reserve Banks, presents a review of recent economic and financial developments—what is happening to prices, unemployment, the balance of payments, interest rates, money supply, bank credit, and so on. Projections are also made for the months ahead. The meeting then proceeds to a discussion among the committee members; each expresses his views on the current economic and financial scene and proposes appropriate monetary policies.

The FOMC directive, embodying the committee's decision on the desired posture of monetary policy until the next meeting, is voted on toward the end of each meeting, with dissents recorded for posterity. If economic conditions are proceeding as had been expected and the current stance of monetary policy is still appropriate, the previous directive may remain unaltered. If conditions change, the directive is modified accordingly.

In recent years, the FOMC directive has usually contained six or seven paragraphs. The first few review economic and financial developments, including the behavior of real output, inflation, monetary aggregates, and interest rates. The fourth or fifth paragraph then turns to a general qualitative statement of current policy goals. For example, at the meeting on 16 November 1982, the goals of the FOMC were set forth as follows:

> The Federal Open Market Committee seeks to foster monetary and financial conditions that will help to reduce inflation, promote a resumption of growth in output on a sustainable basis and contribute to a sustainable pattern of international transactions.

While the statement of goals does not contain everything —we know that the FOMC is not trying to eliminate environmental pollution (at least not yet)—it does include virtually every objective of stabilization policy. This general statement of goals is rarely changed significantly. Toward the end of 1975, for example, when in the throes of recession, the phrase "encouraging economic expansion" replaced "inflationary pressures" as the first goal mentioned.

Immediately following this general statement, the directive presents the long-run target ranges for the monetary aggregates that are thought to be consistent with the broadly stated goals. At the meeting of 16 November 1982, the annual targets were stated as follows:

> The Committee agreed that these objectives would be furthered by reaffirming the (annual) monetary growth ranges . . . 2½ to 5½ percent for M1, 6 to 9 percent for M2, and 6½ to 9½ percent for M3. The Committee agreed that growth . . . around the top of the indicated ranges would be acceptable.

The last order of business in the FOMC directive is to specify the immediate requirements for the implementation of these longer-run objectives. In our by now familiar meeting of 16 November 1982, after noting explicitly that the behavior of M1 over the balance of that year was subject to substantial uncertainty, the Committee stated:

> The Committee seeks to maintain expansion in bank reserves . . . consistent with growth of M2 (and M3) of around 9½ percent at an annual rate from September to December. The Chairman may call for Committee consultation if . . . the related reserve paths are associated with a Federal funds rate persistently outside a range of 6 to 10 percent.

Notice that while the Fed's objectives focus clearly on the monetary aggregates, there is considerable latitude permitted by the target ranges. Moreover, special circumstances can apparently render certain objectives tentative and temporary. It is not surprising, therefore, that in recent years the Fed's accuracy has left much to be desired. Perhaps there are too many numbers and too many targets floating around. It almost guarantees some confusion, as our opening conversation suggested.

With all of this, the manager of the System Open Market Account is expected to conduct open market operations in order to hit reserve and Federal funds rate targets that will produce the desired ranges for the monetary aggregates. Let's first look at the mechanics of open market operations and then return to the overall strategy.

The Operating Room

Open market operations are performed in a well-guarded room within a fortresslike building in the heart of the nation's financial center. The Federal Reserve Bank of New York, designated by the FOMC as its operating arm, is located on Liberty Street only three blocks from Wall Street. This location permits Peter Sternlight, the manager of the Federal Reserve System Open Market Account, to be in close contact with the government securities dealers with whom the Federal Reserve System engages in purchases and sales of securities. Every morning of the workweek he meets with one or more of the securities dealers and gets the "feel of the market," as the opening handshakes (firm or limp? dry or sweaty palms?) telegraph whether the market is likely to be a tick tighter or easier. On occasion Sternlight has been known to shock the market by the judicious use of one of those little hand buzzers (the kind you used to be able to get in novelty shoppes).

Feedback from the securities dealers is only one component of the vast array of data and information marshaled by the account manager in mapping his plans for open market operations on any given day. The starting point, of course, is the directive issued by the FOMC at its last meeting. This expression of the proposed stance of monetary policy, together with the more precise range of desired movements in money market conditions and the monetary aggregates, provide the ultimate target for open market operations. Sternlight must still decide, however, how much to sell or buy, to or from whom, and when.

Money market conditions (particularly short-term interest rates) and monetary aggregates are directly affected by the reserves available to the banking system. Each workday morning, a little after 9:30, Sternlight receives a report on the reserve position of the banking system as of the night before. A sensitive indicator of pressure in this market is provided by the Federal funds rate.

A little later in the morning—but before the 11:15 conference call—the account manager is provided with a detailed projection by the research staff. It covers movements in various items that can affect the reserve position of the banking system—including currency holdings of the public, deposits in foreign accounts at the Federal Reserve Banks, and other technical factors. A change in any of these can cause reserves to go up or down and thereby affect bank lending capabilities, interest rates, and growth in the money supply. For example, as the public cashes checks in order to hold more currency, commercial banks must pay out vault cash and thereby suffer a loss in reserves. As foreign accounts at Federal Reserve Banks increase—that is, as they present checks for payment drawn against commercial banks—reserves of commercial banks are transferred to foreign accounts at the Fed.

A call is also made to the U.S. Treasury to ascertain what is likely to happen to Treasury balances in tax and loan accounts at commercial banks—deposits of the U.S. government generated by tax payments of the public and receipts from bond sales—and to find out what is likely to happen to Treasury balances at the Federal Reserve Banks, from which most government expenditures are made. As funds are shifted from Treasury tax and loan accounts in commercial banks to Treasury balances at the Federal Reserve, the commercial banking system loses reserves.

By 11:00 A.M. Peter Sternlight has a good idea of money market conditions, including what is happening to interest rates, and of anticipated changes in the reserve position of the banking system. He also knows what the FOMC directive calls for. If the FOMC requested moderate growth in reserves in order to sustain moderate growth in the monetary aggregates, and all of the other factors just discussed are expected to pour a large volume of reserves into the banking system, he may decide that open market *sales* are necessary in order to prevent an excessive (more than moderate) expansion in reserves. If, on the other hand, he expects to find reserves going up too little or even declining as a result of these other forces, he may engage in significant open market purchases. It is now clear why knowledge that the Federal Reserve bought or sold so many or so few government securities on a given day or during a given week, in itself, tells us almost nothing about the overall posture or intent of monetary policy.

At the 11:15 conference call with a member of the Board of Governors in Washington and one of the Federal Reserve Bank presidents, Sternlight outlines his plan of action for the day and explains the reasons for his particular strategy. Once his decision is confirmed, the purchase or sale of securities (usually Treasury bills) takes place. The account manager instructs the traders in the trading room of the Federal Reserve Bank of New York to call the thirty-five or so government securities dealers and ask them for firm bids for stated amounts of specific maturities of government securities (in the case of a Fed open market sale) or for their selling price quotations for stated amounts of specific maturities (in the case of a Fed open market purchase). While the Federal Reserve does not engage in open market operations in order to make a profit, it still insists on getting the most for its money, and it is assured of that by vigorous competition among the various dealers in government securities.

It takes no more than thirty minutes for the trading desk to complete its "go-around" of the market and to execute the open market sale or purchase. By 12:30 the account manager and his staff are back to watching the situation and, if necessary, buying or selling additional amounts of government securities to implement the original objective.

Much is left to the judgment of the account manager, even with all of the double-checking with other parts of the Federal Reserve System. By and large, Peter Sternlight receives high marks for his job, despite the errors that inevitably enter any human undertaking. He is also a very pleasant fellow. There are some, however, who would have him, as well as (or especially) the FOMC, replaced by a computer, an automatic telephone, and a disembodied voice that periodically calls out orders to buy or sell $200, $300, or $400 million worth of government securities. The reasons for such an Orwellian prescription for the Federal Reserve are discussed in the next chapter.

Fed Strategy: A Summary

Before ending this chapter let's pause a moment and survey the terrain. After so much on the intricacies of Fed policy making, the details have taken over and we are in danger, to coin a phrase, of losing the forest for the trees.

The ultimate purpose of the Federal Reserve is to influence total spending and GNP. But it has no way of directly altering GNP, so it has to exert its influence indirectly—through the supply of money and credit and various interest rates, mostly medium-term and long-term rates. However, these variables—let's call them the Fed's intermediate objectives— are not directly under the Fed's control either. So the Fed takes aim at so-called *operating targets,* perhaps several different ones, hoping that if it hits these operating targets they will eventually nudge the intermediate objectives and thereby get the job done.

This game plan is illustrated schematically in the accompanying chart. Notice the distinctions between operating targets, intermediate targets and ultimate objectives. Much of the confusion regarding Fed policy arises because these distinctions are ignored.

Notice also what is included in the concepts you will often encounter in the financial pages of your newspaper: the mon-

THE FED'S GAME PLAN

etary aggregates, money market conditions, and the reserve aggregates.

The *monetary aggregates* are intermediate targets; the phrase includes M1, M2, and M3. Other intermediate objectives are bank credit, total credit, and medium-term and long-term interest rates.

Money market conditions are one set of possible operating targets; the phrase refers to free reserves and money market interest rates—especially the Federal funds rate and to a lesser extent the three-month Treasury bill rate.

The *reserve aggregates* are another group of possible operating targets; the phrase includes a wide variety of bank reserve measures, such as the monetary base, total reserves, and so on. The next chart summarizes the arithmetic relationships among the various reserve measures. Interestingly, the last of these—namely, free reserves—is usually considered an indicator of money market conditions rather than as one of the reserve aggregates.

In recent years, as illustrated by the FOMC directive at the beginning of the chapter, the Fed has been putting its plan into operation this way (more or less): It specifies its intermediate objective in terms of a desired range for monetary growth over the year—say an increase in M1 of from 5 to 8 percent. Then it sets an operating target for bank reserves that it figures will produce this rate of monetary growth—say an increase in total reserves or perhaps in nonborrowed reserves of from 4 to 6 percent over the year. Simultaneously, it sets another operating target, the Federal funds rate, that is thought to be consistent with the desired rate of increase in reserves.

The Federal funds rate has been used by the account manager as an indicator of the state of bank reserves. If reserves

---

MONETARY BASE (= total reserves + currency outside banks)
Minus Currency outside banks

= TOTAL RESERVES

Minus member bank borrowing from the Fed

= NONBORROWED RESERVES

Minus required reserves

= FREE RESERVES (or, if negative, NET BORROWED RESERVES)

Relationships Among Alternative Reserve Measures

are growing too rapidly, the Federal funds rate will fall below target, signaling the account manager to intervene and drain reserves by open market sales. Alternatively, if reserves are growing too slowly, the Federal funds rate will rise above target, alerting the account manager to intervene and supply reserves by open market purchases.

Between October 1979 and August 1982 the Federal Reserve shifted its emphasis away from the Federal funds rate as an operating target, turning its attention to reserves instead. But since then, the Fed has returned to its more eclectic ways. And that cannot help but confuse matters for Fedwatchers.

Armed with these details, you can now return to the task of the last chapter: constructing an ideal indicator of Fed policy. If you come up with a winner, let us know.

11

SHOULD A ROBOT REPLACE THE

FEDERAL RESERVE?

Some Monetarists, most notably Milton Friedman, have abandoned countercyclical stabilization policy altogether. They never had any use for fiscal policy to begin with, and the issue of time lags in the impact of monetary policy has led them to jettison countercyclical monetary policy as well. In chapter 5, we noted that time lags do indeed make the implementation of monetary policy potentially hazardous.

"Countercyclical" monetary policy means leaning against the prevailing economic winds: easy money in recessions, to get the economy on the move again; tight money when there is a boom, to slow it down. In its most naive form, however, countercyclical monetary policy tends to ignore the complications bred by time lags.

Assume that the Federal Reserve forecasts a recession due six months from now. If the forecast is correct, and if a current expansion in the money supply would have an impact six months hence, well and good. But what if the Federal Reserve's crystal ball is not that clear, and it is more than a year before the main impact of today's monetary policy is reflected in the economy? Then the effects of today's expansionary monetary policy are likely to be felt *after* the economy has passed the trough and is already on its way up.

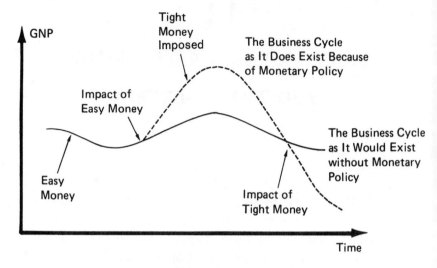

**Friedman's Alleged Perverse Effects of
Countercyclical Monetary Policy**

As the accompanying diagram illustrates, the impact of today's easy money may exacerbate tomorrow's inflation. Tight money will have similarly delayed effects; it may be imposed with the best of intentions, to curtail a boom, but its real impact, being long delayed, might accentuate a recession. Monetary policy is a destabilizer rather than a stabilizer!

On these grounds—the precarious nature of economic forecasting and the alleged length, variability, and unpredictability of the time lags involved—Friedman and some other Monetarists have given up on orthodox monetary policy. Friedman argues that the economy has been and is now inherently stable, and that it would automatically tend to stay on a fairly straight course if only it were not being almost continuously knocked off the track by erratic or unwise monetary policies. Conclusion: quarantine the central bank. The best stabilization policy is no stabilization policy at all. Hasn't it all been said before:

> They also serve who only stand and wait.
> JOHN MILTON

Rules Versus Discretion

What Professor Friedman proposes instead is that the Federal Reserve be instructed by Congress to follow a fixed long-run rule: Increase the money supply at a steady and inflexible rate, month in and month out, year in and year out, regardless of current economic conditions. Set the money supply on automatic pilot and then leave it alone.

The specific rule would depend on the definition of the money supply adopted. Actually, the particular number itself is not so important to Friedman as the restriction that once it is decided upon it be left alone thereafter. No tinkering!

The constant growth rule is intended to keep prices stable and employment high by allowing aggregate demand to grow secularly at the same rate as the growth in the economy's real productive capacity (due to growth in the labor force and increased productivity). It is also supposed to compensate, according to Friedman, for a long-term gradual downtrend in velocity, although, in fact, velocity has done nothing but rise since the end of World War II, and from all indications will continue to do so.

Such a rule, it is claimed, would eliminate forecasting and lag problems and therefore remove what Friedman sees as the major cause of instability in the economy—the capricious and unpredictable impact of countercyclical monetary policy. As long as the money supply grows at a constant rate each year, be it 3, 4, or 5 percent, any decline into recession will be temporary. The liquidity provided by a constantly growing money supply will cause aggregate demand to expand. Similarly, if the supply of money does not rise at a more than average rate, any inflationary increase in spending will burn itself out for lack of fuel. Anyway, any discretionary deviations by the central bank would interfere with the natural course of the economy and only make matters worse.

The United States Congress has been impressed enough to come part of the way toward a Friedman-type rule, in preference to allowing the Federal Reserve to rely entirely on its own judgment and discretion. In March 1975, both the House of Representatives and the Senate passed House Congressional Resolution 133, which instructed the Federal Reserve to "maintain long-run growth of the monetary and credit aggregates commensurate with the economy's long run potential to increase production." It also required that the Fed report quarterly to Congress on its target monetary and credit growth rates for the upcoming twelve months. In November 1977, these provisions were incorporated into the Federal Reserve Act itself.

The Friedman position is based on a number of pillars, each supported by mounds of statistical evidence produced by Friedmanites. However, very little is really known about the length and variability of the time lags. Such evidence as there is, and there is not much, is extremely mixed, as we saw in chapter 5. There is no consensus among economists who have worked in the area.

It is ironic—or instructive—that in the final analysis the extremists from both camps, Monetarist and Keynesian, have collectively ganged up on the Federal Reserve. The extreme Monetarists want to shackle it, because their concern with time lags leads them to believe it is both mischievous and harmful. The extreme Keynesians want to subordinate it to fiscal policy, because they think it is either useless or lethal.

In the middle, squabbling but finding more common cause than they had thought possible, are the moderates: moderate Monetarists, who believe that the forecasting-lag problem is not so great as to negate all the potential stabilizing effects of monetary policy; and moderate Keynesians, who believe that monetary policy probably does change interest rates and/or the availability of credit and that those changes, along with fiscal policy, probably do influence spending decisions in the right way at more or less the right time. While one group concentrates mainly on the money supply and the other primarily on credit conditions, they are nevertheless in agreement that some form of countercyclical monetary policy is, on balance, beneficial.

It seems clear, after all is said and done, that central banking is still at least as much art as science. We simply do not yet know enough to legislate an eternal rule, or even a rule for the next six months, that the Federal Reserve must follow under any and all circumstances. When we do know that much, the Federal Reserve will know it too, and if they are rational they will follow it regardless of whether it has been enacted into law.

Meanwhile, for better or worse, we appear to have no alternative but to rely on our best knowledge and judgment in the formulation of monetary policy. We can only try to make sure that the decision-makers are able and qualified people with open minds and the capacity to learn from experience.

PART IV

*Fiscal Policy
and Debt Management*

12

FISCAL POLICY VERSUS

MONETARY POLICY

The promoter of a match billed as Fiscal Policy versus Monetary Policy would surely be able to call this encounter the Main Event for the Heavyweight Title. Thirty years ago, however, such a contest would not have made even the preliminaries in the Featherweight division. A forfeit would have been declared in favor of fiscal policy. The reason? It was generally believed that monetary policy was unable to defend itself.

The dramatic resurgence of monetary policy since the 1950s rivals the most classic of comebacks. A quarter century ago, monetary policy was relegated to the subservient role of sweeper before the chariot of the Champion. Its functions were to keep bank reserves plentiful and the market for government securities firm, so that interest rates could remain low and nothing impede the right of way of the Great Man. Fiscal policy, alone, in all its glory, would promote full employment, stabilize prices, ensure economic growth, and eliminate poverty. The reader who thinks that this might be an exaggeration, which it probably is, should reread some of the more exuberant literature typical of that era.

Today they march to a different tune. Although some die-hard fans of fiscal policy still decry each move of the monetary authorities, calling every punch a foul and every feint unfair, their enthusiasm is not what it once was and their ranks have dwindled with the passage of time. Government economists now place monetary policy on an equal footing with fiscal policy in the pursuit of national economic objectives. Some academic economists even go so far as to argue that monetary policy should be *the* instrument of economic stabilization, that the impact of fiscal policy is negligible, at best. As we indicated earlier, much of the controversy centers about the debate between the Monetarists and the Keynesians.

How Fiscal Policy Works

According to the Monetarists, a change in the money supply will alter aggregate spending and GNP by a predictable amount, since the velocity of money is quite stable. Thus they contend that monetary policy is a much more effective instrument than fiscal policy.

Keynesians, on the other hand, are skeptical about the reliability of the relationship between the money supply and GNP. As they view it, a change in the money supply can alter aggregate spending only to the extent that it first changes interest rates or the availability of credit, and then only if business or household spending is sensitive to those changes. There is no direct link between the money supply and spending. Put briefly, the relationship between the money supply and GNP is seen as tenuous and variable, since fluctuations in the velocity of money may counteract changes in its supply.

In Keynesian eyes, changes in government spending or

taxation—the primary tools of fiscal policy—*do* have a direct and fairly predictable impact on GNP. An increase in government spending raises GNP immediately. It also induces additional "multiplier effects" via a GNP-consumption-GNP link. As GNP rises because of an initial injection of government expenditure, consumers receive more income; they spend a fraction of this increased income, which causes GNP to go up even further. For example, if government spending rises by $10 billion, income (or GNP) automatically goes up by $10 billion. Of this larger income, consumers will then spend a predictable fraction, say four-fifths, or $8 billion. Since spending by A is income to B, GNP goes up by this $8 billion as well. Of this, consumers then spend another four-fifths, or $6.4 billion. By now, GNP has gone up $24.4 billion. Eventually this process will come to a halt as the successive increments in income and spending become smaller and smaller; but the end result will be an increase in GNP by some multiple of the original increase in government spending.

Changes in tax rates are seen as having a similar multiple impact on GNP. If tax rates are lowered, consumers are left with more disposable income. They spend a predictable fraction of this, causing a rise in GNP, which in turn induces additional consumer expenditure. Conclusion: to bring about an expansion in spending and GNP, we should increase government spending and/or lower tax rates, that is, create a budget deficit. Anti-inflation policy would call for the opposite: reduce government spending and/or raise tax rates, that is, create a budget surplus.

It is important to note the central role of this GNP-consumption-GNP relationship in the Keynesian "multiplier" analysis. If consumer spending does not respond to changes in income, tax-rate changes would not affect spending or

How to Score (Old-Timers' Day)

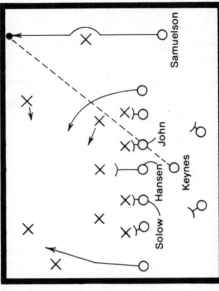

Monetarist Power Sweep

Milty Friedman hands off to J. S. Mill—who streaks down the right sideline behind a big block (actually a clip) by Swifty Irving Fisher that completely upends Big Tommy Malthus.

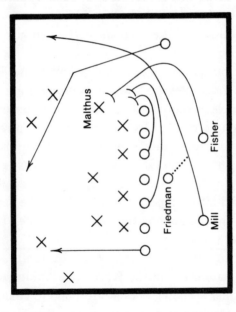

Keynesian Long Bomb

J. M. Keynes hits Poor Paul Samuelson with a TD pass—fantastic blocking by the unsung heroes of the front line, led by Bob Solow, Alvin Hansen, and Elton John (betcha didn't know he was a closet Keynesian).

economic activity and the "multiplier effects" would be minimal.

Changes in government spending and/or tax rates can be implemented in many different ways. Government spending can be changed via military expenditures, outlays for education, urban renewal, farm price supports, medical research, the space program, or for any other specific government program. Tax receipts can be altered by changing the corporate income tax, the personal income tax, the investment tax credit, or any specific excise or sales tax.

While the impact of a change in any one of these tax or expenditure categories can be made virtually identical with a change in any other one, insofar as the arithmetic effect on GNP is concerned, profound social implications flow from which particular tax or expenditure program is or is not altered. For example, if we are experiencing substantial unemployment and a low rate of economic growth, and fiscal policy is decided upon as the appropriate remedy, a choice arises between lowering taxes and raising government spending. If we lower tax rates, the expansion in GNP will be brought about by private spending. On the other hand, if we increase government spending, this will give us more government services as well as more private purchases. Which alternative we choose should depend on the volume of government (social) services we want.

Going still further: If we decide that we should increase government spending, should it take the form of more money devoted to curbing environmental pollution or an expansion in the MX missile program? When we are faced with inflationary pressures, should we cut back military expenditures or antipoverty programs? These issues involve social problems and policies that go far beyond the bounds of economics.

Measuring Fiscal Policy

Until now, we have discussed expansionary and contractionary fiscal policy in terms of deficits and surpluses in the federal budget. A budget deficit is expansionary and a budget surplus is contractionary. However, just as many widely used indicators of monetary policy are less than adequate (see chapter 9), so also are there serious limitations to using the *current* deficit or surplus as a guide to the stance of fiscal policy.

The measurement problem stems from the fact that tax receipts, and hence the size of the deficit or surplus, vary passively with GNP. Congress sets tax *rates,* not receipts; receipts then go up and down with GNP. Given the level of government spending, when GNP rises tax receipts automatically increase and surpluses are automatically created (or deficits reduced). When GNP falls tax receipts decline and deficits automatically result. Thus, it is impossible to draw any meaningful conclusions regarding the stance of fiscal policy by comparing a budget surplus in one year at one level of GNP, with a deficit in another year at a *different* level of GNP.

For example, the existence of a deficit during a recession suggests, at first glance, that fiscal policy is expansionary.It may be, however, that the tax structure is so steep that it drives income (and thereby tax receipts) down to recession levels. A deficit may thus actually be the result of a *contractionary* fiscal policy.

The budget concept that *is* useful as an indicator of the posture of fiscal policy is called the full employment budget. The main problem in comparing deficits or surpluses in year X with year Y is that there are different levels of GNP in both years. As the accompanying diagram indicates, the idea of the full employment budget eliminates this problem by sticking to one concept of GNP, namely the full employment GNP. The full employment budget is defined as what the federal budget surplus (or deficit) *would be,* with the expected level of government spending and the existing tax structure, *if the economy were operating at the full employment level of GNP throughout the year.*

This calculated measure, the full employment budget, can be used to evaluate the effects and the performance of fiscal policy more meaningfully than the actual state of the budget, whatever it might be. Indeed, as an indicator of fiscal policy, the full employment budget is a much less ambiguous policy measure than any we thus far have been able to produce for monetary policy.

As an illustration, the diagram indicates that the actual level of GNP produces a poor tax harvest and, consequently, a deficit in the actual budget. Nevertheless, fiscal policy is hardly expansionary. In fact, it is quite the opposite; the diagram shows that if GNP had been at the full employment level, or close to it, tax revenues would have risen so greatly that the *full employment budget* would have had a substantial surplus. Conclusion: The fundamental stance of fiscal policy is restrictive, not expansionary.

A reduction in tax rates swings the tax receipts line (in the diagram) downward and diminishes the full employment surplus. An increase in government spending also shrinks the full employment surplus. A tax-rate increase or a drop in government spending, both of which are restrictive actions,

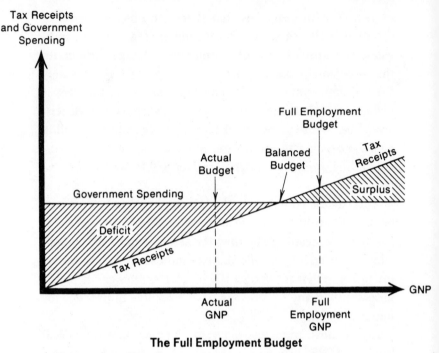

The Full Employment Budget

enlarge it. Thus, it is clear that changes in the full employment budget reflect basic *discretionary* changes in fiscal policy, as contrasted with movements in the actual budget that can be the *passive* result of fluctuations in GNP. In fact, an expansion in GNP due to a tax cut could succeed in lowering the size of the actual deficit.

All of this violates the most sacred canons of "traditional" (or pre-Keynesian) finance. According to the maxims of "orthodox" finance, an actual deficit is a signal to immediately set about balancing the budget by *raising* tax rates and/or *decreasing* government spending—this promptly drives GNP lower, thereby creating an even *larger* deficit, which makes matters worse all around.

Financial Aspects of Fiscal Policy

The fiscal policy mechanism just described is not the whole story. This is recognized by both Keynesians and Monetarists. The total impact on GNP of an expansionary fiscal policy cannot be fully ascertained until the method of financing government deficits is specified. Similarly, the net effect of a reduction in government spending and/or increases in tax rates cannot be fully calculated until the disposition of the surplus is taken into account.

When GNP goes up as the result of deficit spending, the public's need for day-to-day transactions money rises along with it. If the supply of money does not increase simultaneously, the public will find itself short of cash, will presumably sell off some financial assets in order to try to get additional money, and will thereby drive up interest rates. This so-called "crowding out" effect may inhibit private investment spending and home-building, partly offsetting the expansionary impact of the government's spending.

But a budget deficit can be financed in either of two ways. For one, the government might simply print money to finance itself. Since this is often frowned upon in the best of circles, its twentieth-century equivalent is used instead: the Federal Reserve buys the bonds that are sold by the government and in the process brand-new checking accounts are created for the government. If this is done, the increased supply of money will probably be sufficient to satisfy the enlarged need for money and interest rates will not rise. In this case, there will be little or no offset to the expansionary impact of the deficit spending, and GNP will be able to rise without interference from the monetary side.

Alternatively, the deficit might be financed by the sale of government securities to the public. If this is done, however, the pressure on financial markets is actually intensified, since the increase in the supply of new bonds on the market drives up the rate of interest even further. The sale of government securities will "crowd out" private borrowers, and the consequent decline in investment spending will offset an even larger portion of the increased government spending. The net effect, according to the Keynesians, is still expansionary, although less so than in the case of money-financed deficits.

In any event, regardless of details, the important point is that the execution of fiscal policy is inextricably mixed up with monetary implications. The two cannot be separated.

The Monetarists Versus the Keynesians

The Keynesian position is that any fiscal action, no matter how it is financed, will have a significant impact on GNP. Keynesians do not deny that interest rates are likely to rise as GNP goes up, unless new money is forthcoming to meet cash needs for day-to-day transactions. Thus, they admit that a deficit financed by money creation is more expansionary than one financed by bond sales to the public, and that both are more expansionary than increased government spending financed by taxation. However, Keynesians do not believe that the decrease in private investment spending caused by higher interest rates (the "crowding out" effect) will be great enough to offset fully the government's fiscal actions. They think that the net impact on GNP will be significant, and in the right direction, regardless of what financing methods are used.

One reason for this conclusion is that higher interest rates are seen as having dual effects. They may reduce private investment spending, but they may also lead people to economize on their cash balances, thereby supplying part of the need for new transactions money from formerly idle cash holdings. Put somewhat differently, even if a deficit is not financed by new money, the velocity of existing money will accelerate (in response to higher interest rates) so that the old money supply combined with the new velocity will support a higher level of spending and GNP.

The Monetarist view, on the other hand, is that unless a budget deficit is financed by new money creation it will not alter GNP significantly. In order for GNP to rise, the money supply must expand. If a fiscal deficit is financed by printing money, it will indeed increase spending and GNP. But according to the Monetarists, it is not the deficit that is responsible—it is the additional money. Furthermore, a deficit is a very clumsy way to go about increasing the money supply. Why not simply have the Federal Reserve engage in open market operations? That would accomplish the same purpose, a change in the money supply, without getting involved in budget deficits or surpluses.

As the Monetarists see it, a fiscal deficit financed in any other way—as by selling bonds to the public—will leave GNP largely unaffected. True, the government will be spending more. But others will wind up spending less. The "crowding out" effect is extremely powerful. Net result: little change in total spending or in GNP. The rise in government spending will *initially* increase GNP. However, this will increase the demand for cash for transactions purposes and drive interest rates up, and bond sales to finance the government's expenditures will drive rates up still further. The public will be buying government bonds and financing the government, instead of buying corporate bonds and financing business firms. The rise in interest rates will reduce private investment spending by as much as government spending is increased, and that will be the end of the story. Government fiscal policy, unaccompanied by changes in the supply of money, merely changes the proportion of government spending relative to private spending.

Anti-inflationary fiscal policy encounters similar objections from the Monetarists. An increase in tax rates that generates a fiscal surplus reduces private income and consumer spending. If the government destroys or simply holds the money, the tax revenues it has collected over and above its expenditures, then the surplus is accompanied by a reduction of the money supply in private pockets. Both Keynesians and Monetarists would agree that this is anti-inflationary, although for different reasons—the Keynesians because of the direct fiscal impact on consumer spending, with the tax increase reducing people's take-home pay, and the Monetarists because of the contraction in the money supply.

But if the government uses the surplus to retire part of the national debt, the funds flow back into the economy. The government retires debt by buying back its bonds. Bond prices are driven up, interest rates fall, and private investment spending increases. Keynesians would argue that GNP will still decline, that the debt retirement is a minor ripple on a huge wave. Monetarists, however, would say that private investment spending will increase until it replaces the cutback in consumer spending, leaving no net effect whatsoever on GNP.

As we stressed in chapter 4, the confrontation between fiscal and monetary policy can be decided only by resort to empirical evidence. The accompanying figure shows the simulated response in nominal GNP (left side) and real GNP (right side) to a $10 billion expansion in government expenditure based on the Federal Reserve's model. In each of the pictures there are three lines, each representing alternative monetary policies accompanying the expansionary fiscal policy. The solid line shows the effect with a monetary policy that keeps the three-month Treasury bill rate unchanged. That assumption implies an expansion in the money stock to accommodate rising demand as GNP goes up. The dotted line assumes a monetary policy that keeps bank reserves (but not necessarily the money supply) unchanged. The dot-dash line simulates the results with a constant money stock.

It is evident from the pictures that this last monetary policy causes a substantial amount of crowding out, as we would expect. The fixed money stock policy forces rates of interest to rise as GNP increases and this cuts off investment spending. Note, however, that there isn't complete crowding out of nominal GNP, although in the right-hand picture there is complete crowding out of real GNP after about two years.

The multiplier effects of government spending are much more expansionary with the two more accommodating monetary policies. Thus the Fed model confirms the crucial role of money for the size of the fiscal policy multipliers. But the Fed model maintains that complete crowding out does not take place even with a fixed money stock assumption.

The original Monetarist model of the Federal Reserve Bank of St. Louis is less wishy-washy than its sparring partner: An increase of $1 billion in the money supply raises GNP by over $5 billion after one year, while a similar increase in government spending has *zero* impact on GNP over the same time period. An increase in government spending

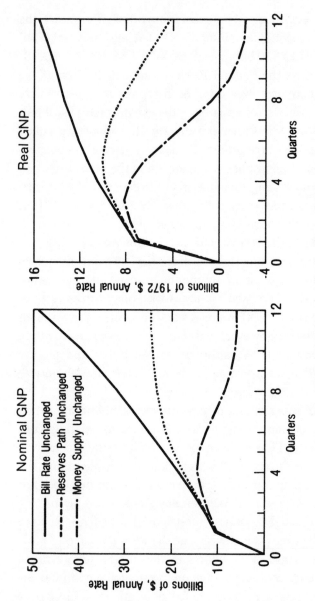

Evidence of Crowding Out from the Federal Reserve Model

raises GNP after six months, but by the time a year has elapsed, other types of spending have been crowded out to offset the expansion in government expenditures. What other types of spending? On this the St. Louis model is silent, just as it is silent on the transmission mechanism through which money affects spending. Indeed, it is this agnosticism on the transmission process and the surprising result with respect to fiscal policy that make the St. Louis model incomprehensible to many Keynesians.

Who gets the verdict has implications far beyond flattering the egos of economists with vested intellectual interests on opposite sides of the fence. If we are in a recession and use easy money to raise GNP, interest rates will fall and private investment and home building will expand. On the other hand, if we use fiscal policy—lowering tax rates or increasing government spending—consumer spending or social services will be favored instead.

If we are in a boom and want to reduce aggregate spending, tight money will hit housing hard; tight fiscal policy probably will not. If a vibrant housing industry is important for national social and economic welfare—on the theory that the American Dream consists of each citizen owning his own house with a well in the backyard—perhaps we should rely mainly on easy money to stop recessions and mainly on tight fiscal policy to halt inflation.

A rational overall stabilization policy would evaluate all of these elements, and more, before embarking on a course of action. There are likely to be other side effects, some desirable, others undesirable. Often political considerations will be involved as well. It is difficult, for example, to raise taxes in an election year. Not to mention the influence that various pressure groups, both business and labor, are likely to bring to bear on such decisions.

In any case, the importance of *both* fiscal and monetary policy, and the numerous interrelations between them, make it plain that there can be no clear-cut winner. If either fiscal policy or monetary policy is declared the victor, to the neglect and subjugation of the other, it is we who will be the losers.

13

SHOULD WE WORRY ABOUT

THE NATIONAL DEBT?

"Personally," said President Eisenhower, in his State of the Union Message in 1960, "I do not feel that any amount can properly be called a surplus as long as the nation is in debt. I prefer to think of such an item as a reduction in our children's inherited mortgage."

In the same vein, Senator Harry F. Byrd, Sr. pondered the $275 billion national debt in 1955 and gloomily predicted: "The debt today is the debt incurred by this generation, but tomorrow it will be debt on our children and grandchildren, and it will be for them to pay, both principal and interest."

Debt worriers are fond of statistical computations. We now have a national debt of some $1,300 billion (in the form of marketable and nonmarketable government securities, held by the public and by government agencies) and a population of about 235 million. Conclusion: every man, woman, and child in this country owes about $5,530 whether they know it or not. Every newborn infant starts life not only with a pat on the back but also with a $5,530 share of the national debt hanging over his or her head.

Agonizing over the size of the public debt is one of our major national preoccupations. Is the situation really all that bad? Are the debt worriers right when they warn us that, by passing on a national debt of $1,300 billion, we are burdening future generations with a weight that will be almost impossible for them to bear? Are they correct in cautioning us, with stern voices, that we are penalizing those as yet unborn by forcing them to pay for our own vices and follies?

The National Debt Equals the National Credit

The national debt is essentially the net result of past and present fiscal policy, mostly past. It is the sum of all past deficits, less surpluses, in the federal budget. A budget deficit requires that the government either print money or borrow to cover the deficit, and most modern governments choose to borrow (that is, sell government securities). As a result, we acquire a national debt, embodied in the form of government bonds; the total of government securities outstanding *is* the national debt. It is increased by every additional deficit we incur and finance by issuing more bonds.

If the national debt is a debt, we must owe it to someone. Indeed we do—we owe it mostly to ourselves. Most of our government's bonds are internally held, that is, they are owned by citizens of the United States. Thus, while we the people (as the United States) *owe* $1,300 billion, we the people (as owners of government securities) are simultaneously *owed* close to the same amount. A government bond is, after all, an asset for whoever buys it.

All evidences of debt must appear on *two* balance sheets, and government securities are no different from any other IOU in this respect. Every IOU appears on the balance sheet of the debtor, as a liability; but it also turns up, not surprisingly, on the balance sheet of whoever is holding it, its owner, this time as an *asset*. Thus, every liability necessarily implies the existence of a financial asset owned by someone else. For the same reason, every *financial* asset implies a corresponding liability on the part of someone else.

This accounting gem has interesting ramifications. It means, for one, that merely creating money cannot, in and of itself, make a country richer, a conclusion that always pleases conservatives. After all, money is a financial asset, which implies that somewhere else there is a corresponding liability. If liabilities go up as rapidly as assets, the country as a whole (including both the government and the private sector) can be getting no richer.

Most of our money is in the form of checking accounts, which are liabilities of financial institutions. The part of our money that is in the form of coin or currency is a liability of either the United States Treasury or the Federal Reserve, depending on which agency issued it.

Thus merely creating money can hardly make a nation richer, no matter how much it creates. To become richer—to increase its net worth—a country must increase its output of *real* assets, its production of real goods and services. As conservatives like to point out, if we want to become wealthier, we must work harder and produce more. Creating money, per se, will not do it.

By the same token, however, exactly the same logic also implies that another favorite conservative incantation is equally false: namely, the belief that increasing the national debt makes a country poorer. Government bonds are liabilities of the government but are financial assets to whoever owns them. If the national debt increases, someone's financial assets go up as much as the government's liabilities. If domestically held assets rise along with liabilities, the country as a whole can be getting no poorer.

The very term *national debt* is thus a half-truth. If it is a domestically held debt, it could just as well be called the *national credit.* Both labels are half-truths. As with all liabilities, it is *both* a debt (to the borrower) *and* a credit (to the lender).

To become poorer—to reduce its net worth—a country must reduce its holdings of real assets, curtail its production of *real* goods and services. Increasing the national debt, no matter how high, cannot in and of itself make a country poorer so long as it is owned internally. (Actually, about $200 billion of our $1,300 billion national debt is held by foreign citizens and institutions.)

Nor does an increasing national debt, just because of its size, impose a burden on future generations. As long as the debt is held internally, neither the interest nor the principal represents a dead weight on the backs of our children and grandchildren. The taxes that must be raised to pay the interest are merely transfers from one group within the economy, the taxpayers, to another group, the bondholders. Future generations inherit tax liabilities, but they also inherit bonds and the right to receive the interest on them.

Even if the debt had to be paid off, future generations, as inheritors of the bonds, would be making payments of the principal to themselves. In fact, of course, the federal debt never has to be fully repaid any more than does the debt of any going concern, public or private. As parts of the debt come due, they can be repaid with fresh borrowings. Continuous refinancing is typical of the modern successful corporation, because confidence in the company's ability to earn future income makes holding its bonds both safe and profitable. Similarly, confidence in the continuing viability and taxing power of the federal government eliminates the need for net repayment of principal, either currently or in the future.

The Real Burden of the Debt: I

Does this mean, then, that the debt worriers are completely off the track? Not quite, and therein lies the story of the *real* burden of the debt as contrasted with the imaginary burden.

In the first place, holdings of government bonds are not evenly distributed among the population. Some of us have more than our $5,530 share, much more; and some have less, much less. Thus current interest payments on the debt, while "only" an internal transfer from taxpayers to bondholders, may create problems of legitimate concern to the public. If taxpayers are largely from the lower and middle income groups, while bondholders are primarily in the upper income brackets, then the tax collection → interest payment transfer will increase the inequality of income distribution. Relatively little is known about the pattern of interest payments on the government debt according to income of the recipient. This transfer *may,* therefore, interfere with social objectives of reducing income inequality.

Furthermore, if the federal debt grows at a faster rate than GNP, tax rates may have to be increased in order to meet interest payments. Higher tax rates may reduce work incentives. If so, production falls and overall economic well-being decreases. In the United States, however, the national debt has actually declined, quite substantially, as a proportion of our gross national product. In 1945, the national debt was about 130 percent of GNP; in 1955, 70 percent; in 1965, 45 percent; and in 1982 it was 42 percent.

Even if the debt falls as a proportion of GNP, if interest *rates* go up sufficiently then tax rates may have to be raised to meet the interest payments, thus again possibly reducing work incentives. Interest rates have indeed risen since 1945, but nevertheless the interest "burden" (interest charges as a proportion of GNP) has not increased substantially. Over the past thirty years, annual interest payments have been stable at between 1½ and 3 percent of GNP, with the most recent figure hovering at 2.8 percent.

The Real Burden of the Debt: II

Aside from the possible income-redistribution and work-incentive problems associated with interest payments on the national debt, there is one way in which the debt might impose a burden, a cost, on future generations. This involves not the interest, but the principal itself.

As we noted previously, a country will become poorer only if it reduces its output of real assets, its ability to produce real goods and services. In this very meaningful sense the wealth of future generations can be measured by the real capital stock they inherit, the real productive capacity of the economy we bequeath to them. A smaller capital stock permits less production, hence less consumption. A larger capital stock enables the economy to produce more, hence consume more.

Assume that the economy is already operating at a full capacity rate of production and that the budget is balanced. Whereupon the government increases its spending, financing its additional expenditures by sufficient new *taxation* to forestall inflation. In this case, the increased use of resources by the government comes primarily at the expense of consumption. Consumers, left with less after-tax income, have to cut back their spending by as much as government spending has been stepped up.

Alternatively, under the same initial circumstances, assume that the additional government spending is *debt-financed* rather than tax-financed, and that a tight monetary policy is used along with debt-financing to prevent inflation. Now interest rates will rise and the increased use of resources by the government will come primarily at the expense of investment instead of consumption. The higher interest rates will release resources from private investment for use by the government, with investment spending cut back by as much as government spending has been increased.

As a result, the production of new plant and equipment will be curtailed, and future generations will consequently inherit a smaller capital stock. Future productive capacity is lower than it might have been. In this limited sense, the "burden" of debt-financed current government expenditure is transferred to future generations.

Two qualifications are necessary. First, note that the argument assumes we start from a full capacity rate of production, roughly a full employment level of GNP. If the additional government spending were to take place during a recession, when there are idle resources available, then there would be no "burden" on future generations, no matter how it was financed. During a recession there are unemployed resources that can be tapped, so the government can increase its spending without anyone else reducing theirs. There would be no reason to permit a rise in interest rates, since the danger of inflation would be minimal, and an expansion in spending and GNP would be beneficial to all.

Under such circumstances, the future capital stock is not diminished. In fact, if the government's deficit spending succeeds in getting us out of the recession, the future capital stock will probably be *enlarged.* Thus increasing the national debt during a recession, instead of imposing a burden on future generations, is actually doing them a favor.

Second, the "burden" argument totally ignores what the government spends the money on. Assuming full employment, if the government's expenditure is for current consumption purposes—such as subsidizing inexpensive lunches for congressmen or schoolchildren—then total capital passed on to the future is indeed reduced. But if the government builds highways or dams, or increases any type of capital asset that raises future productivity, the increased investment by the government replaces the decreased investment by private business. Future generations will inherit the same capital stock, except more will be in the form of public capital and less in the form of private capital.

The Nuts and Bolts of Debt Management

Given a national debt of $1,300 billion, its day-to-day management has implications for the functioning of financial markets and for economic stability. How can the debt be refinanced most smoothly when portions of it come due? How much of the debt should be in the form of short-term Treasury bills, how much in the form of long-term Treasury bonds?

The dimensions of the Treasury's debt-management chore can best be appreciated by realizing that about $400 billion of the debt comes due every year and must be paid off. How? By refinancing it, of course, that is, by borrowing $400 billion from someone else. The Treasury can replace the maturing issues with new short-term Treasury bills, or with intermediate- or long-term bonds, thus providing some elbow room for altering the maturity structure of the debt.

What are the objectives of day-to-day debt management? One goal is to minimize the interest cost of the debt to the taxpayers. But this can hardly be the only objective. If it were, the Treasury could minimize the interest cost—indeed, reduce it to zero—by simply printing money and buying back all the outstanding securities. That is, it could replace its interest-bearing debt (bills and bonds) with its noninterest-bearing debt (money). Obviously, the Treasury does not "monetize the debt," because to do so would probably result in massive inflation, and the Treasury also has the objective of managing the debt to promote economic stability.

These two objectives often dictate opposite policy actions. Minimizing the interest cost suggests that when we are in a recession, and interest rates are low across the board, the Treasury should refund its maturing issues with new long-term bonds, thus ensuring low interest payments for itself well into the future. During boom periods, on the other hand, when interest rates are typically high, the Treasury should refinance by selling short-term issues, Treasury bills, so the government does not have to continue paying high rates after yields have fallen to more normal levels.

Stabilization objectives call for just the opposite policies. When we are in a recession, the last thing we want to do is to raise long-term interest rates, which is precisely what pushing long-term securities onto the market is likely to accomplish. Boom periods, when we *do* want to raise long rates, are when we should sell long-term bonds.

Thus the objective of minimizing interest costs dictates lengthening the maturity structure of the debt (more long-term bonds relative to short-term bills) during recession periods and shortening the maturity structure during boom periods. For purposes of economic stabilization we should do the opposite—try to shorten the maturity structure during recessions and lengthen it during prosperity.

Debt-management policy must be administered in coordination with monetary and fiscal policy. If minimizing the interest cost is the primary goal of the Treasury, then monetary and fiscal policy will have to take appropriate action to offset this counterstabilization debt policy. If economic stabilization is the primary objective of debt management, then the monetary and fiscal authorities can take this into account and reduce the forcefulness of their own actions.

Monetary policy, fiscal policy, and debt management are often considered the three primary tools of stabilization policy. In practice, however, debt management has typically been the runt of the litter. Perhaps that is just as well. Given the power of monetary and fiscal policy to implement national economic goals, perhaps debt management can make its most significant contribution by successfully accomplishing the more limited but not unimportant task of continuously refinancing a very large volume of government securities without unduly disturbing the nation's financial markets.

PART V

Of Stocks and Intermediaries

14

DOES MONETARY POLICY AFFECT

THE STOCK MARKET?

Any civic or social club program chairperson knows that if it is announced that next week's meeting will feature a renowned speaker on "Environmental Pollution," hardly anyone will show up. But if the announcement states that the topic will be "The Outlook for the Stock Market" and mentions a speaker no one ever heard of, the hall will be packed. It would be hard to find a subject that intrigues people more than the stock market. Everyone knows about stocks: how they go up, and how they can make you rich. Fifty years ago everyone knew about stocks: how they go down, and how they can make you destitute.

Why do stock prices go up and down? Not so much particular stocks, like IBM or Xerox, but why does the entire stock market soar or shudder, with all stocks more or less rising or falling together?

It is a fact of life that the total supply of stocks in existence is more or less fixed. What changes is not so much the number of shares lying around—in vaults, under mattresses, and concealed between the pages of the family Bible—but the price of each.

For example, at the end of 1982 the market value of all the publicly held shares of stock in existence amounted to something like $1,750 billion. In the early 1960s it was about $500 billion, and in the early 1950s less than $200 billion. And yet in the past thirty years corporations have raised relatively little money by issuing new stock, perhaps $200 billion or so at most. This means, and the word has obviously gotten around, that almost all of that $1,750 billion—probably at least $1,500 billion of it—represents price appreciation of existing shares.

The fact that the total supply outstanding is relatively fixed does not, of course, imply that the amount offered on the market need be fixed. People who have bought, and even some who haven't, can always sell. Thus in recent years stocks have been drifting out of the hands of individual investors, who on balance have been selling, into the plush suites of institutional investors, who have been buying. In 1960 pension funds, mutual funds, insurance companies, and other institutional investors held about 15 percent of the market value of outstanding shares; now they hold about 30 percent. But 70 percent is still held by individuals, about 25 million of them, and each and every one is out to make a killing.

Strangely enough, given the widespread interest in the stock market, economists have generally had very little to say about it. The most popular postwar college textbook, Paul Samuelson's *Economics,* is estimated to have sold over three million copies since it first appeared in 1948. Considering the royalties accruing to so popular an author, and a leading economist in the bargain, one would think he might have accumulated both the wherewithal and the trained experience to discover at long last the secret of what makes the market tic. But if Paul has found out, he isn't telling! The latest edition of *Economics* contains only 9 pages (out of 861) on the stock market.

Some economists are less reticent than Professor Samuelson about letting us in on why stock prices fluctuate. Their explanations have ranged from the influence of sun spots on people's emotional behavior to the conspiratorial machinations of shadowy figures in high places. However, the explanations that are of most interest to us here deal with money and monetary policy.

Is it true, as some claim, that the elusive clue to movements in overall stock prices is found in changes in the money supply? Or does the secret lie, as others believe, in changes in monetary policy in general? If the former are correct, and to some extent the latter, perhaps all the paraphernalia with which market analysts now so laboriously wrestle for signs of the future can be put aside; the best tout sheet might turn out to be the weekly bank reserve statistics.

A Money Supply View of Stock Prices

The belief that fluctuations in the money supply provide the key to movements in stock prices is based on a series of cause-and-effect hypotheses that contain elements of both Monetarist and Keynesian thinking. In its simplest form, the reasoning is as follows: when the Federal Reserve increases the money supply at a faster than normal rate, the public, finding itself with more cash than it needs for current transactions, spends some of its excess money buying financial assets, including stocks. Since the supply of stocks is more or less fixed, especially in the short run, this incremental demand raises their price. Some stocks will go up more than others and some may go down, depending on the prospects for particular companies, but overall the *average* of stock prices will rise.

Or the transmission process might be somewhat more complex, but with similar results. The increase in the money supply may first lead the public to step up its *bond* purchases, thereby raising bond prices. Higher bond prices mean lower interest rates. With bonds yielding less, some potential bond purchasers are likely to switch over to the now relatively more attractive stock market. The demand for stocks expands because their substitute, bonds, has become more expensive—just as the demand for Yamahas will expand when their alternative, Hondas, become more expensive (not to mention the Suzuki).

Or it could be an even more roundabout process. The larger money supply leads to lower interest rates, more investment spending (creating more household income and thereby more consumer spending), a higher GNP, and, along with it, larger corporate profits. Enlarged corporate profits spur stock purchases and higher stock prices.

In any case, the result is the same. Whether the chain of causation is direct, from the money supply to stock prices, or indirect, through the bond market and interest rates, or through GNP, an increase in the money supply at a faster than normal pace is seen as accelerating the demand for stocks, leading to higher stock prices.

Conversely, decreases in the money supply—or increases at a slower rate than necessary to provide for the transactions needs of a growing economy—leave the public with shortages of funds. Result: among other things, a cutback in stock purchases—again, either directly or because, with higher interest rates, bonds become more attractive buys, or because corporate profits decline as GNP falls. This reduced demand for stocks lowers their prices.

Conclusion: a rapidly expanding money supply leads to higher stock values; inadequate monetary growth leads to a falling market.

Persuasive as the underlying reasoning seems, all too frequently the facts simply do not bear it out. Evidently, too many other crosscurrents simultaneously impinge on the stock market, such as business expectations and political developments. Like so many other single-cause explanations in economics, this simplified view of stock price determination contains too much truth to ignore but not enough to make it very reliable in the clutch.

Consider 1929, and the couple of years before and after. From mid-1927 to mid-1928, the money supply increased by 1.6 percent; from mid-1928 to mid-1929, it increased by 1.2 percent. The stock market, meanwhile, going its merry way, *doubled.*

In the next two years, from mid-1929 to mid-1931, the money supply contracted by about 5 percent each year. If the stock market was merely reacting to changes in the money supply it was by all odds the biggest overreaction in history, because the proverbial bottom dropped out and the market promptly lost all the gains it had made in the previous two years and then some.

Furthermore, it is not at all clear precisely what is cause and what is effect. Did the market crash in 1929 because, among other things, the money supply contracted? Or did the money supply contract because the market crashed (as banks called speculative margin loans, and checking accounts were wiped off the books)? The latter explanation is as logical as the former.

The 1929 stock market collapse, as many see it, was due to a number of interrelated factors: an unwarranted mood of euphoric optimism prior to the crash, excessive speculative activity, fundamental weakness in underlying business conditions, and so on. The money supply, if it influenced the break at all, did so only as one among many causes.

None of which is meant to imply that the money supply was or is unimportant. If it had been rapidly and forcefully restored to its 1929 level by 1930, or even 1931, the depression initiated by the stock market collapse would probably not have been either as severe or as long as it turned out to be. That the Federal Reserve stood by, wringing its hands, while the money supply declined by 30 percent from 1929 to 1933 undoubtedly intensified and prolonged what we now call the Great Depression. But that is a very different thing from saying that movements in the money supply caused or could have given one even a vague idea of the heights or the depths to which stock prices went from 1927 to 1931. As a matter of fact, most of the drop in the money supply occurred *after* 1931; by that time, however, the market was too weary to do much reacting, either over or under.

To come closer to the present, in 1940 the stock market fell 15 percent even though the money supply was then rising 15 percent (on top of a similar rise the year before). In 1962, again, the market tumbled despite an increasing money supply. And in 1973–74 the stock market fell by more than 40 percent, even though the money supply increased by 11 percent over that two-year period.

On other not infrequent occasions, however, it is true that declines in stock prices *were* preceded or accompanied by declines in the rate of growth of the money supply, as in 1957, 1960, 1969, and 1981. And often increases in stock prices were indeed associated with increases in the growth of the money supply, as in 1967, 1968, 1975, and 1982.

In at least some of these instances, however, both stock prices and the money supply might conceivably have been

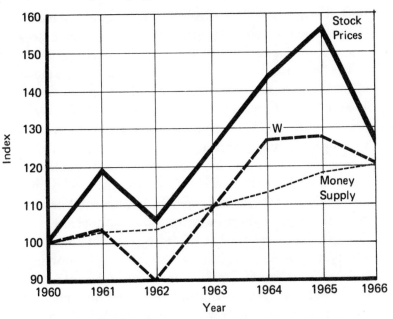

Stock Prices and Other Variables, 1960–1966

reacting to a third causal force, perhaps an upturn in business conditions stimulated by the outbreak of war or peace, a spurt in consumer spending, or something else. An improvement in business conditions, regardless of cause, typically leads to an expansion in business loans at banks, a larger money supply, brighter profit prospects, and thereby higher stock prices. As the history of business cycles indicates, such upswings (or downturns) are capable of generating a cumulative push that can work up considerable momentum, carrying *both* the money supply and stock prices along with it.

The accompanying chart provides some idea of the pitfalls involved in reading a cause-and-effect relationship into two sets of statistics simply because they move together. The thick line indicates the movement of stock prices, annually, from the end of 1960 through the end of 1966, using stock prices at the end of 1960 as the base (= 100).

The thin dashed line, on a similar index basis, is the movement of the money supply annually, also from the end of 1960 through the end of 1966. Over this particular six-year period, changes in the money supply clearly bore little relationship to turning points in stock prices.

Finally, the chart also includes a third line (W). Its movements are obviously closely related to changes in stock prices. Almost without exception, the line labeled W and the line tracing stock prices move up and down together.

Cause and effect? The line labeled W, make of it what you will, is an annual index (1960 = 100) of the number of times members of the old Washington Senators baseball team struck out each year, over the period 1960 through 1966. (Source: The Sporting News's *Official Baseball Guide and Record Book,* Annual, 1960–66.) For at least those years, evidently, an investor trying to forecast turning points in the stock market would have been better off spending time reading the box scores instead of the money supply figures.

Monetary Policy and Wall Street

Once we expand our horizon to encompass more than the money supply alone, however, there is agreement that monetary policy, *in general,* frequently does have a considerable influence on the stock market. It is by no means the only influence and is often overshadowed by other forces and events; nevertheless, it is widely believed that on balance monetary policy has had a substantial effect on stock prices at times in the past, especially since the mid-1960s, and is likely to continue to do so in the foreseeable future.

This is quite aside from the power of the Federal Reserve to set margin requirements on stock purchases. In an attempt to prevent a repetition of the speculative wave, financed heavily with borrowed funds, that carried the market to dizzy heights until the fall of 1929, Congress in the 1930s authorized the Federal Reserve to impose margin (or minimum downpayment) requirements on the purchase of stocks. If the margin requirement is 100 percent, then 100 percent cash must be put up and no borrowing at all is permitted. If the margin requirement is 80 percent, that much of one's own cash must be put up when buying a security and only the remaining 20 percent can be financed by borrowing from a bank or a broker. Of course, you could always finance the entire amount by borrowing from your brother-in-law and no one would be the wiser (except perhaps, in the long run, your brother-in-law).

High margin requirements probably have helped restrain speculation in stocks, particularly by those who could least afford it. Nevertheless, if the Federal Reserve had only this device to influence the market, it would be relying on a weak reed indeed. Margin requirements are 100 percent at Santa Anita and Hialeah racetracks, but at last report speculative activity by those who could not afford it as well as by those who could appeared unimpaired.

The impact of overall monetary policy on stock prices stems not so much from the Federal Reserve's power to set margin requirements as from its influence over the money supply, the entire spectrum of interest rates and financial markets, current and expected business conditions, and, last but far from least, the expected rate of inflation. It is in the recent past, rather than thirty or forty years ago, that the effects of monetary policy on stock prices are most clearly visible. The credit squeezes of 1966, 1969, 1974, and 1981 are prime examples—stock prices tumbled in each of those episodes.

Indeed, these events appear to have impressed so many in recent years that expectations about the immediate future course of monetary policy have now become one of the main topics of conversation among stock market analysts. Every week stock market participants eagerly await the release of the Federal Reserve's money supply figures, fearful of making commitments without this knowledge in hand.

If the figures show that the money supply is growing *faster* than the Fed's announced guidelines—say the Fed is aiming to increase the money supply by 4 to 6 percent annually, but the weekly figures reveal that in fact it has been increasing by 9 percent—then Wall Street concludes that the Fed will *soon be tightening* to get the money supply back on track.

Alternatively, if the figures show that the money supply is growing *more slowly* than the Fed's announced guidelines—again, say the Fed is aiming to increase the money supply by 4 to 6 percent, but this time the weekly figures reveal that in fact it has been increasing only by 1 percent—then Wall Street concludes that the Fed will *soon be easing* to get the money supply back on the track.

Views on Wall Street are mixed as to precisely what such figures imply for stock prices. If the money supply has been growing faster than the Fed's target, so that *tightening* is in order, then some see this as heralding a fall in stock prices, but others view it as signaling an upturn. Those who see tighter money as precipitating a fall in the stock market reason that tighter money means higher interest rates (lower bond prices); this will make bonds relatively more attractive than stocks, resulting in lower stock prices as well. On the other hand, others see tighter money as signaling an *upturn* in stock prices on the logic that inflation has been bad for stock prices; tighter money will stop inflation, which in turn will eventually bring interest rates down and thereby stimulate higher stock prices.

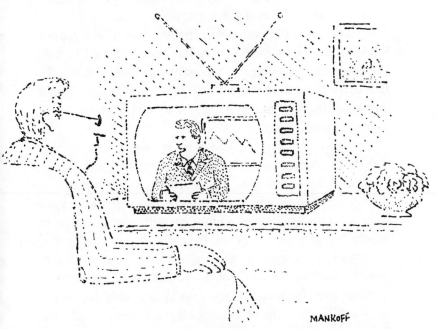

"On Wall Street today, news of lower interest rates sent the stock market up, but then the expectation that these rates would be inflationary sent the market down, until the realization that lower rates might stimulate the sluggish economy pushed the market up, before it ultimately went down on fears that an overheated economy would lead to a reimposition of higher interest rates."

Drawing by Mankoff; © 1981 *The New Yorker Magazine, Inc.*

The same divergence of views exists for the implications of easier money. If the money supply has been growing more slowly than the Fed's target, so that *easing* is in order, some see this as likely to produce higher stock prices. They reason that easier money means lower interest rates (higher bond prices); this will make stocks relatively more attractive than bonds, resulting in higher stock prices. Others, however, come to the opposite conclusion. They see easier money as fueling inflation, which in turn will eventually bring higher interest rates and thereby depress stock prices.

By and large, the first group (tighter money will depress stock prices, easier money stimulate them) seemed to hold the predominant opinion in the early seventies. But as inflation accelerated during the decade, the second group gained adherents (tighter money will stimulate stock prices, easier money depress them).

Both groups, however, had their problems (and so have we). One problem is difficulty in interpreting the weekly Federal Reserve statistics, which are often ambiguous. One money supply measure may overshoot the target at the same time as another money supply measure undershoots it. Which measure should be used? Or the money supply may overshoot the target on the basis of the past week's or month's data but undershoot it on the basis of the past two or three months' data. Which time span should be used?

Not to mention the potentially biggest problem of all: The Federal Reserve may have changed its money supply target. There is a one-month lag between meetings of the Federal Reserve's Open Market Committee and release to the public of what transpired. If the Fed changed its target from a 4–6 percent annual growth rate to 1–3 percent, then 1 percent is right on target and does not imply future easing. Someone who acts as though it does imply future easing could be making a serious mistake.

But then whoever said making money in the stock market is easy! The lesson is that Fed watching is helpful in anticipating stock market trends, but is no short cut to getting rich because too many other things are simultaneously affecting stock prices.

15

WHAT IS FINANCIAL

INTERMEDIATION?

Financial intermediation played an important role, it is said, in permitting monetary velocity to rise during the 1950s. Financial *dis*intermediation, on the other hand, has been a significant factor in aggravating periodic tight money conditions. The words are big, but the process, it turns out, is commonplace and familiar. It is so ordinary, in fact, that we can add to those who have been talking prose all their lives, and were not aware of it, the millions who have been engaged in some aspect of financial intermediation or disintermediation, and did not realize it.

Financial intermediaries are nothing more than financial institutions—such as commercial and savings banks, savings and loan associations, credit unions, pension funds, insurance companies, and the like—that act as middlemen, transferring funds from ultimate lenders to ultimate borrowers. They borrow from Peter in order to lend to Paul.

We will examine financial institutions in some detail in the following chapter. Regardless of the details, however, what all financial intermediaries have in common is that they acquire funds by issuing their own liabilities to the public (savings deposits, savings and loan shares), and then turn around and use this money to buy financial assets (stocks, bonds, mortgages) for themselves.

Because these institutions exist, savers who do not want to

hoard their cash under a mattress, but who feel hesitant about purchasing corporate bonds or stocks or mortgages because they feel that these assets are perhaps too risky or too illiquid, are given a third alternative. They can "purchase" savings deposits or savings and loan shares. In that way, they can hold a relatively safe and quite liquid financial asset, yet still earn *some* interest income. At the same time, corporations and potential home-owners can still sell their bonds, stocks, and mortgages to the financial intermediaries rather than to the original savers themselves. Financial intermediaries, in brief, "intermediate" between original savers and final borrowers.

Financial intermediation is precisely this process: savers depositing funds with financial institutions rather than directly buying bonds or mortgages, and the financial institutions, in turn, doing the lending to the ultimate borrowers.

*Dis*intermediation is the reverse: savers taking funds out of deposit accounts, or reducing the amounts they normally put in, and investing directly, in their own names, in market securities such as stocks and bonds.

Financial Intermediation Lowers Interest Rates

Interest rates on securities (bonds, stocks, mortgages, and so forth) must compensate lenders for the risks inherent in owning them—risks such as potential capital losses due to interest rate fluctuations, possible default, illiquidity, and so on. Financial institutions are in a better position than individuals to bear and spread these risks of security ownership. Because of their large size, intermediaries can diversify their portfolios and minimize the risk involved in holding any one security. They are experts in evaluating borrower credit characteristics. They employ skilled portfolio managers and can take advantage of administrative economies in large-scale buying and selling.

For these reasons, they can afford to receive lower yields on their assets and will accept them if they have to. Competition among financial intermediaries forces interest rates to the lowest level compatible with their evaluation of the risks of security ownership. These yields are lower than if the same securities were held by individual investors, unable to minimize their risks so efficiently.

Looked at another way, financial institutions also help to reduce the demand for money, thereby contributing to lower interest rates. People hold money both for day-to-day transactions and for safety because of the riskiness of stock or bond holding (relative to cash). But such intermediary liabilities as savings deposits and savings and loan shares are also safe, as safe as money and virtually as liquid. Indeed, they are so safe and liquid that they are often called near-monies or money substitutes.

With such safe and liquid assets available and earning interest to boot, people will have less desire to hold money itself. They can be almost as liquid (and also earn some interest) if they substitute savings deposits in place of some of their cash holdings. The money that people release and deposit in financial intermediaries will be used, in turn, by the intermediaries to buy bonds, mortgages, and so on. Thus additional money enters the bond market and bond prices are bid up (interest rates drop). The net effect of financial intermediation is to lower interest rates.

The growth in financial intermediaries has been spectacular in the last thirty years. Time and savings deposits in commercial banks have grown from $30 billion at the end of World War II to over $1,000 billion, and savings and loan shares have increased from less than $10 billion to over $600 billion. At the same time we have experienced a general *increase* in the level of interest rates. This does not necessarily contradict what we have said previously. If all other factors had remained the same, the growth in intermediation should have reduced interest rates. But, of course, all other factors have not remained the same.

Both the money supply and intermediary liabilities have been growing, providing us with increased liquidity. However, this has been more than absorbed by the rise in GNP, which has increased the demand for cash for transactions purposes. The net effect has been that the increase in the demand for liquidity has outpaced the increase in the supply of liquidity, so that interest rates have risen. In light of the great rise in GNP since World War II, what is surprising, and must be attributed in large part to the growth of intermediation, is that the rise in interest rates has not been considerably greater.

It is worth noting that since financial intermediation tends to lower interest rates, or at least moderate any increase, it has been highly beneficial to our rate of economic growth. A high rate of economic growth requires a large volume of real investment. The lower the rate of interest that ultimate borrowers must pay, the greater their expenditure on real investment is likely to be.

The beneficial effect of intermediation on economic growth can also be seen from the viewpoint of risk bearing. Intermediaries are better able than individuals to bear the risks of lending out capital. As was previously stressed, ability to diversify, economies of scale, and expertise in lending account for this comparative advantage of institutions over individuals. As financial intermediaries own a larger and larger portion of the marketable securities outstanding, the subjective risk borne by the economy is lowered, interest rates are reduced, and more real investment takes place. Funds are channeled from ultimate lenders, through intermediaries, to ultimate borrowers more efficiently than if the intermediaries did not exist.

Intermediation and Monetary Policy

One of the earliest confrontations between modern Monetarists and Keynesians arose during the 1950s. It focused on the influence of financial institutions, such as savings and loan associations and savings banks, on the efficacy of monetary policy. Since savings deposits could not have checks written on them at that time, they were not part of the narrowly defined money stock (M1). But they seemed sufficiently close to checking accounts to warrant the question: Should monetary policy be concerned with such nondemand deposit liabilities of financial intermediaries in gauging the impact of monetary policy?

Recent changes in regulations have blunted some of the debate. Some savings deposits now have direct checking privileges while others can be automatically transferred to checking accounts. The distinctions between commercial banks, savings and loans, and savings banks are less pronounced than they once were. Nevertheless, the controversy survives in the form of the various definitions of money that we encountered back in chapter 2. Let's go to the original source of the debate and then see what lessons can be drawn.

John G. Gurley and Edward S. Shaw of Stanford University wrote a series of articles in the mid-1950s that eventually became known as the Gurley-Shaw thesis. They emphasized that the deposit liabilities of savings and loan associations, savings banks, and other financial intermediaries are, after all, not much different from the demand deposit liabilities of commercial banks, even though we generally call only the latter "money." It is true that we can spend demand deposits, and that we cannot spend a savings and loan share without cashing it in first. But cashing it in is a simple matter, easily accomplished; thus savings and loan shares and savings deposits, whether at commercial banks or at savings banks, are for all practical purposes almost as liquid as demand deposits.

Gurley and Shaw conclude that since these near-monies are outside the jurisdiction of the Federal Reserve, they make the successful execution of monetary policy difficult. Controlling liquidity only through the narrowly defined money supply will not work very well, since liquidity can also be provided by near-monies. For example, assume the Federal Reserve reduces the narrowly defined money supply to inhibit spending on real and financial assets to help fight inflation. Interest rates on securities rise. Now the intermediaries go into action. Aware of the higher yields and the profits they imply, savings and loan associations raise the rate they offer on deposits in an effort to attract more funds, which they can then invest in the higher-yielding securities. The increase in deposit rates induces some individuals to put more funds in savings banks, savings and loan associations, and so on. Financial intermediation shifts into high gear.

The individuals switching money to the intermediaries may use funds they formerly had invested directly in securities, thus rebuilding their liquidity; they also may use what were idle money balances, now coaxed out of hiding by the attractive rates posted and widely advertised by the intermediaries. As long as the latter occurs to some extent, there will be a net expansion in the demand for market securities (by the intermediaries), a consequent moderation in the rise in interest rates, and—most important of all—the channeling of previously idle money balances into the eager hands of ultimate borrower-spenders.

The behavior of financial intermediaries therefore partially offsets the impact of monetary policy on interest rates. Rates still rise as a result of tight money, but less than they would have without the intermediaries. The Fed has difficulty in controlling inflation because it can't control nonbank financial intermediation and the creation of near-monies.

The Gurley-Shaw hypothesis, first developed in the mid-1950s here and at about the same time in England by the Radcliffe Committee, seemed vindicated by the experience of the 1950s and early 1960s. At that time, tight money invariably was accompanied by the mobilization of idle balances, an expansion in intermediation by financial institutions other than commercial banks, and consequent financing of the boom by these intermediaries. Focus on broader definitions of money, such as M2 or M3, seemed justified. Moreover, debate raged as to whether the Federal Reserve should have the power to set reserve requirements for savings banks and savings and loan associations, and congressional hearings were held to explore ways to solve the problem.

Legislation along these lines was finally enacted in 1980. The Depository Institutions Deregulation and Monetary Control Act, otherwise known as the Banking Act of 1980, requires both savings and loans and savings banks to hold reserves against their checking account and business time deposit liabilities, as specified by the Federal Reserve; as a *quid pro quo*, they have full access to temporary borrowing from the Federal Reserve when needed.

But even before this legislation, the dire Gurley-Shaw prognosis regarding the efficacy of monetary policy had been blunted by deposit rate ceilings under Regulation Q. In fact, the effects of Regulation Q have been so pervasive they deserve special treatment of their own.

Deposit Rate Ceilings

The Federal Reserve sets the legal maximum interest rates, through what is known as Regulation Q, that commercial banks are allowed to pay on their time and savings deposit liabilities. The maximum interest rates that savings banks and savings and loan associations may offer depositors are also regulated.

During the tight money episodes of the 1970s and 1980s, Regulation Q reversed the predictions of Gurley and Shaw. Tight money was accompanied by financial *dis*intermediation rather than financial intermediation. During these periods money market interest rates rose, but unlike during the 1950s and 1960s deposit interest rates were held down by a restrictive Regulation Q. With deposit interest rates substantially below open market rates, savers stopped moving funds *into* financial institutions, instead, they moved them *out*. People took money out of savings accounts and put funds directly into money market instruments and other primary securities, thereby bypassing the intermediaries. This behavior is known as financial disintermediation.

Disintermediation put the intermediaries under severe

pressure. With substantial withdrawals and minimal inflows of new funds, their profit position was threatened, their solvency was endangered, and their ability to lend evaporated.

The disintermediation effects of Regulation Q have been softened in the past few years by several regulatory changes. In 1970 the Federal Reserve eliminated the rate ceilings on large-size ($100,000 and over) negotiable Certificates of Deposit (CDs) that mature in less than three months. And in 1973 the Fed eliminated the ceilings on longer-maturity large-size CDs as well.

Equally important, especially in minimizing disintermediation during the tight-money episode of 1978–79, was a newly permitted six-month money market time certificate that commercial banks and thrift institutions were allowed to issue starting in mid-1978. The interest rate on these is tied to the Treasury bill rate, so that depositors can receive high money market yields without withdrawing their funds from the depository institutions. They can merely shift their funds for six months in the same bank or savings and loan association from a passbook savings account to a money market time certificate.

Since Regulation Q complicated life for everyone during the 1970s and early 1980s, how did it get started in the first place? It was enacted in the Banking Act of 1933, on the ground that excessive interest rate competition for deposits during the 1920s had undermined the soundness of the banking system. It was believed that competition among commercial banks for funds had driven deposit rates up too high. To cover costs, banks acquired high-yielding but excessively risky low-quality assets. This deterioration in the quality of bank portfolios, it was said, contributed to the collapse of the banking system in the early 1930s. Abolition of interest rate competition for deposits, by setting legal rate ceilings, was seen as rooting out the basic element weakening the banking system.

In retrospect, it is not at all clear that the historical experience which led to Regulation Q was correctly interpreted at the time. Interest rates on bank time and savings deposits actually declined during the 1920s, and thorough investigation since has failed to substantiate any appreciable deterioration in the quality of bank assets during that period.

Regulation Q has effectively prevented aggressive, well-managed banks from offering depositors more attractive interest rates than the bank next door. Aggressive banks that would like to compete for funds by bidding more for deposits have been legally prohibited from doing so, which also means, of course, that depositors have simultaneously been deprived of the enlarged options that more vigorous price competition among banks would offer them.

The Banking Act of 1980 promised to put an end to Regulation Q. The Act established a Depository Institutions Deregulation Committee which is to gradually phase out interest rate ceilings on time and savings deposits and eliminate them entirely by April 1, 1986. In fact, the Act did put an end to the ban against paying interest on checking deposits by permitting all depository institutions to offer NOW accounts, which are in effect interest-bearing checking accounts. But don't cheer too soon: Congress could always change its mind at the last minute, as it has done so often in the past.

16

THE STRUCTURE OF THE FINANCIAL

SERVICES INDUSTRY

In chapter 15 we saw what financial intermediation is all about. Since savers are often wary of buying stocks, bonds, or mortgages, because they consider these assets too risky or illiquid, they acquire instead the relatively safe and liquid deposits of financial institutions. In turn, the financial institutions buy the stocks, bonds, and mortgages. Financial institutions can minimize the risks involved better than individuals because their size enables them to diversify their portfolios more easily and because they have experts who can better evaluate the riskiness of various financial assets.

In this chapter we will take a broad look at each type of financial intermediary. We are most interested in exactly how these institutions *intermediate* between saver-lenders and borrower-spenders. So we will pay special attention to the *composition* of their liabilities and assets, because they acquire funds from saver-lenders by "selling" their own liabilities, and then turn around and obtain earning assets when they disperse the funds to borrower-lenders. By paying a lower interest rate when they acquire funds than they charge when dispersing them, financial institutions hope to make a profit on the differential.

Financial Institutions in Profile

Although all financial institutions have a lot in common, there are also substantial differences among them. Ranked in terms of asset size, for example, as in the accompanying table, commercial banks are easily the largest. In addition to sheer size, the composition of liabilities and assets also differs significantly from one type of financial institution to another.

1. *Commercial banks* are the most prominent of all financial institutions. There are about 15,000 of them, ranging from the Bank of America, with over $100 billion in deposits, to thousands of small banks scattered throughout the country, many of which have less than $5 million in deposits. They are not only the largest but also the most widely diversified in terms of both liabilities and assets. Their

Financial Institutions, Ranked by Asset Size (end of 1982)

Institution	Asset Size*
Commercial banks	$1,625
Savings and loan associations	720
Life insurance companies	564
Private noninsured pension funds	337
State and local government retirement funds	254
Sales and consumer finance companies	231
Money market mutual funds	207
Property and casualty insurance companies	204
Mutual savings banks	181
Credit unions	85
Mutual funds	85

*Total financial assets, in billions of dollars.
SOURCE: Federal Reserve Flow of Funds Accounts.

major source of funds used to be demand deposits, but in the past two decades savings and time deposits, including certificates of deposits, have become even more important than demand deposits.

With these funds they buy a wide variety of assets, ranging from short-term government securities to long-term business loans and home mortgages. They are prominent lenders in virtually every financial market.

2. *Savings and loan associations* (S&Ls) have traditionally acquired almost all their funds through savings deposits, usually called shares instead of deposits, and used them to make home mortgage loans. This was their original purpose —to encourage family thrift and home ownership. For the most part, S&Ls are still oriented in these directions, but changes are taking place rapidly. The Banking Act of 1980 —formally known as the Depository Institutions Deregulation and Monetary Control Act of 1980—granted them the power to issue checking accounts (usually called NOW—for negotiable order of withdrawal—accounts) and also to make consumer loans.

There are about 5,000 savings and loan associations in the United States, extending from coast to coast. They encountered serious problems in recent years because such a large proportion of their liabilities is in the form of savings deposits, which in effect are payable on demand, while so many of their assets consist of long-term mortgages, a lot of them acquired years ago when interest rates were much lower.

Typically they pay an interest rate of say 6 percent for their savings deposits and then turn around and make home mortgage loans at a higher rate, say 10 percent. The 4 percent differential is supposed to cover their operating costs and yield a profit. However, imagine the problems they face when short-term interest rates rise to say 14 percent: they are caught in a profit squeeze because they have to pay 14 percent to get new money (and also to prevent an outflow of their existing deposits), while their assets are still earning 10 percent (or even less) because most of them were acquired long ago.

3. *Mutual savings banks* are practically identical with savings and loans except that there are only about 500 of them and they are concentrated mostly on the East Coast. Both are often called "thrift institutions." As their name implies, mutual savings banks are legally structured as "mutuals" or "cooperatives," with depositors or shareholders "owning" the institution.

Like S&Ls, they have traditionally obtained most of their funds in the form of savings deposits and used the money mainly to make home mortgages. However, the Banking Act of 1980 also gave them the power to issue interest-bearing checking accounts (NOW accounts) and to make consumer and some business loans.

Since mutual savings banks are so similar to S&Ls, they face identical problems when interest rates rise. They have to pay more to get new money, and to retain a lot of what they have, but the return they get on most of their assets fails to rise correspondingly since these are long-term mortgages acquired years ago.

4. *Life insurance companies* rank third in asset size, right after commercial banks and S&Ls. They insure people against the financial consequences of death, receiving their funds in the form of periodic payments (called premiums) that are based on mortality statistics. They can predict with a high degree of actuarial accuracy how much money they will have to pay out in benefits this year, next year, even ten or twenty years from now. They invest accordingly, aiming

for the highest yield consistent with safety over the long run. Thus a high percentage of their assets is in the form of long-term corporate bonds and long-term mortgages, although the mortgages are typically on commercial rather than residential properties.

5. *Pension and retirement funds* are similar to life insurance companies in that they are mainly concerned with the long run rather than the short run. Their inflow of money comes from working people building a nest egg for their retirement years. Like life insurance companies, pension and retirement funds are able to predict with a high degree of accuracy how much they will have to pay out in pensions (called annuities) for many years into the future. Since they face few short-term uncertainties, they mainly invest in long-term corporate bonds and high-grade stocks.

6. *Property and casualty insurance companies*, on the other hand, are more likely to encounter short-run liquidity needs. They insure homeowners against burglary and fire, car owners against theft and collision, and business firms against negligence lawsuits, among other things. With the premiums they receive—big ones from car owners under twenty-five years old—they buy high-grade municipal and corporate bonds, high-grade stocks, and short-term money market instruments (for liquidity).

7. *Sales and consumer finance companies* specializing in lending money for people to buy cars and take vacations and for business firms to help them finance their inventories. Many of them, like the General Motors Acceptance Corporation, are owned by a manufacturing firm and lend money mainly to help retailers and customers buy that firm's products. Others, like Household Finance and Beneficial Finance, mainly make small consumer loans. They get their funds by selling their own short-term IOU's (called commercial

paper) to business firms with funds to invest for a short while, as well as by selling their own long-term bonds.

8. *Credit unions* are generally included, along with S&L's and mutual savings banks, in the category of "thrift institutions." There are over 20,000 of them, some in every state in the Union, most quite small but a few with assets exceeding $1 million. They are organized as cooperatives for people with some sort of common interest, such as employees of a particular company or members of a particular labor union or fraternal order or church. Credit union members buy shares, which are the same as deposits, and this makes them eligible to borrow from the credit union.

Until recently credit unions offered only savings deposits and made only consumer loans. Like S&Ls and mutual savings banks, however, they have had their powers broadened considerably by the Banking Act of 1980. They can now offer checking accounts (called credit union share drafts) and also make long-term mortgage loans.

9. *Mutual funds* are almost exclusively stock market-related institutions. Pooling the funds of many people of moderate means, the fund's management invests the money in a wide variety of stocks, thereby obtaining diversification that individuals acting alone probably could not achieve. Shareholders can always redeem or sell back their shares if they wish, but the price they'll receive from the fund depends on what has happened to the stocks it holds. Buying shares in a mutual fund is thus much more risky than buying a savings deposit or a money market instrument, like a Treasury bill, but it is less risky than buying stocks on your own.

10. *Money market mutual funds* are something else again. They are the growth phenomena of the 1970s and early 1980s. From only $2 billion in 1974 they exploded to $45 billion by 1978 and then to a startling $200 billion by

1982. They are like the old-fashioned kind of mutual fund, described above, in that people buy shares in a fund. However, the fund's management does not invest the money in the stock market. Instead, it is put into highly liquid short-term money market instruments, such as large-size bank negotiable CDs, Treasury bills, and high-grade commercial paper.

Financial Institutions Are Becoming More Alike

Our list suggests that there are at least ten different types of financial institutions in the United States. In fact, the distinctions have deep historical and institutional roots. But in recent years the differences have been eroding, making depository institutions increasingly alike. By the year 1990 it will difficult to tell them apart.

For instance:

1. Traditionally, checking accounts have been the exclusive province of commercial banks, with other deposit-type institutions legally barred from offering checking facilities. In the 1970s, however, thrift institutions began offering NOW accounts, which are just checking accounts under another name. The Banking Act of 1980 confirmed their right to do so, with the result that now S&Ls, mutual savings banks, and credit unions all offer some type of checking account. Even money market mutual funds have gotten into the act, though they are not mentioned in the Banking Act of 1980.

2. Traditionally, only commercial banks made business loans and savings banks specialized in mortgage lending,

credit unions in consumer loans. However, the Banking Act of 1980 enlarged the lending powers of all the thrifts, so that now S&Ls and savings banks can make consumer and business loans and credit unions can make mortgage loans.

The net result of all these changes is that the traditional specialization of financial institutions is breaking down. Financial institutions are becoming more general and more alike. In a sense, they are all in the process of becoming commercial banks—dealing in checking accounts as well as savings deposits and becoming more diversified in their assets as well as their liabilities.

Securities Brokers, Investment Bankers, and the Glass-Steagall Act

Neither securities brokers and dealers nor investment bankers are listed as major financial institutions in the table at the beginning of this chapter, because they have relatively small amounts of assets of their own. However, they are crucially important as intermediaries in the distribution and trading of huge amounts of securities, including corporate stocks, bonds, state and local government securities, and U.S. government securities.

The difference between investment bankers on the one hand and brokers and dealers on the other involves the distinction between *primary* and *secondary* securities markets. Primary markets refer to the sale and distribution of securities when they are *originally issued* by the money-raising corporate or government unit. Secondary markets involve the *subsequent trading* of those securities once they are already outstanding. The New York Stock Exchange is an example of a secondary market.

Investment bankers operate in primary markets, selling and distributing new stocks and bonds directly from the issuing corporations to their original purchasers. Brokers and dealers are involved in secondary markets, trading "used" or already outstanding securities.

The difference between brokers and dealers is that brokers do not buy or sell for their own account. They are pure middlemen, matching buyers and sellers of a particular security and earning a commission fee for bringing the two together. Dealers, on the other hand, "take positions" in securities: they buy them for their own account hoping to resell at a higher price. If they are wrong, and the price falls before they can unload, their hoped-for profit becomes a loss instead.

Many of the nationwide stock exchange firms, like Merrill Lynch, act in all these capacities. They are called stockbrokers, or brokerage houses, because they act as agents in executing orders to buy or sell securities on the various stock exchanges. At times they also act as dealers and at other times as investment bankers.

Our main interest at the moment, however, is in the ways in which a number of large stock exchange firms have branched out in the last few years to provide new kinds of financial services that used to be considered beyond their province. Merrill Lynch was the innovator, starting the ball rolling in 1977 with its Cash Management Account (CMA). The CMA consists of a financial package that includes a credit card, instant loans, check-writing privileges, investment in a money market mutual fund, and complete record keeping, including monthly statements. This brings brokerage houses close to being in the banking business. Can banks respond to the challenge by turning around and going into the securities or money market fund business themselves? So far the answer is no, and the reason they can't is called Glass-Steagall.

The Banking Act of 1933, known as the Glass-Steagall Act, separated commercial banking and investment banking, where the latter refers specifically to issuing, underwriting, selling, or distributing new stock and bond offerings of corporations. Commercial banks had become deeply involved in the sale and distribution of new stock and bond offerings in the 1920s, not always with happy results. There were suspicions that banks on occasion dumped new offerings into trust funds that they managed because they couldn't sell them to anyone else. To avoid such conflicts of interest, the Banking Act of 1933 divorced commercial from investment banking. Banks involved in both areas were forced to choose one or the other.

Commercial banks are still permitted to distribute new offerings of federal government securities and "full faith and credit" general obligations of state and local governments. But Glass-Steagall forbids them to get involved in new offerings of corporate stocks or bonds or municipal revenue bonds. Revenue bonds differ from general municipal obligations in that they are not backed by the full taxing power of the state or local government; bondholders have a claim only on the revenues of the specific project financed, such as a toll road or a state university dormitory (maybe even yours). The Act has also been interpreted as meaning that commercial banks cannot offer mutual funds, including money market mutual funds.

Commercial banks believe they are being discriminated against by the provisions of the Glass-Steagall Act. After all, securities firms and investment bankers—not to mention life insurance companies—have penetrated their deposit and checking account business via money market mutual funds and CMAs, but commercial banks can't penetrate the securities business with stock or money mutual funds or by distributing new municipal revenue bonds or new corporate securities of any sort.

In light of the breakdowns in barriers separating financial institutions that have occurred over the past decade, it is likely that new legislation in the 1980s will carry that trend even further and permit commercial banks to gain a foothold in the securities business. When that takes place, the financial services industry will have escaped the legacy of the 1930s legislation that has shaped its development during the past fifty years.

PART VI

Money and National Priorities

17

FINANCIAL RESOURCES,

REAL RESOURCES,

AND NATIONAL PRIORITIES

As the United States has encountered serious social problems in the past decade, many have urged that we need a major reordering of our national priorities. What is being said is that we have to do something to alleviate poverty, urban blight, crime, pollution, and so on. Typically, that is the end of the story, except for apocalyptic visions of what is likely to happen if *something* isn't done. No attempt is made to quantify what has to be done, however.

What dollar amounts are involved? Who will foot the bill? Priorities are by nature relative; if some are raised higher, then mustn't others be dropped lower? Should a reordering be accomplished via tax changes or selective credit policies?

Quantifying Reordered Priorities

Aside from the direct reduction of poverty, which we shall return to later, there appears to be widespread concern about the need to: (a) improve mass transit in urban and suburban areas; (b) curb environmental pollution; (c) provide better housing for low-income families; (d) improve police protection, law enforcement, and the judicial and penal systems generally; (e) upgrade the quality of education, particularly that available to minority group children; and (f) better the quantity and quality of medical research and health care, especially by increasing its availability to the aged and to low- and middle-income groups.

It has become abundantly clear that none of these problem areas can be resolved simply by spending more money. It is equally true, however, that improvements cannot realistically be expected unless more money is indeed spent. At present, estimates of the dollar amounts needed to make significant headway in these areas are little more than guesswork (and even less thought has been devoted to least-cost methods of realizing objectives). Nevertheless, some crude calculations can give a rough idea of the financial magnitudes involved. Take out your pencil, because here come some numbers.

Conservative estimates require the following *additional* spending: $10 billion a year (1982 prices) to improve mass transit; $23 billion a year more to make meaningful progress toward pollution control; $23 billion a year more for low- and middle-income housing; $29 billion additional annually for law enforcement and judicial-penal reform; $35 billion annually toward nationwide school reform; and another $35 billion a year for appropriate health care and medical research. This package adds up to a total of $155 billion *a year* more for these purposes than we, as a nation, are currently spending.

How does this stack up against existing priorities? In 1982, for example, 64 percent of our $3,060 billion national output was in the form of consumer goods and services, 11 percent was capital goods (business investment spending), and 6 percent went for federal defense. These are the Favored Priorities: they command 81 percent of our total output of goods and services. The remaining 19 percent of GNP are the Ugly Duckling Priorities—state and local government spending (13 percent), housing (3 percent), and federal nondefense purchases of goods and services (3 percent).

Almost all of the $155 billion a year, or 5 percent of 1982's GNP, needed to *reorder* priorities falls into the Ugly Duckling class—in the main, they are either state and local government functions, housing, or federal government nondefense functions (either by tradition or because of default on the part of the private sector). A meaningful reordering of national priorities implies taking *5 percent* of our national output away from the Favored Priorities and moving it over to the Ugly Ducklings. A real reordering of priorities, as opposed to liberal lip service, is clearly no trivial matter.

A Growth Dividend

Some advocates of reordering priorities think that it can be done with little pain, that a normal "growth dividend" will magically supply all the needed $155 billion. They are not altogether wrong. Growth will help, but alone it is not enough. As economists have observed time and again, there is no such thing as a free lunch—you always wind up paying for it, in some way.

Economic growth refers to the ability of our economy to expand its productive capacities over a period of time. Most forecasts for the coming decade anticipate a real growth rate averaging no more than about 3.3 percent a year. If realized, this would yield additional real output averaging about $100 billion a year every year during the rest of the 1980s. But the process of growth does no more than make about $100 billion

of additional resources available every year, which are then up
for grabs. If state and local spending, housing, and federal
nondefense spending—the Ugly Ducklings—continue to receive the same shares of the pie as they do now, which total 19
percent, then growth alone will provide only 19 percent of the
$100 billion annual expansion in output for those purposes, or
an incremental $19 billion a year every year.

At best, then, a growth dividend could contribute only $19
billion the first year, $38 billion the next year, $57 billion the
year after that, and so on. It would take more than eight
years to reach the requisite $155 billion, and by that time
neglect would have swollen the required amount. While we
may not preach "instant gratification," neither do we en-
dorse "benign neglect."

Deliberate Resource Reallocation

If we are truly to reorder priorities, we thus have no choice
but deliberately to use governmental policies to *reallocate*
some resources. If the Ugly Duckling Priorities are to get
more, some of the Favored Priorities will have to get less.
The only questions are what to cut and by how much.

A favorite starting point for radical surgery is usually
business plant and equipment spending. Let the giant corporations pull in their belts; aren't they already too big? Hit the
Fat Cats where it hurts, below the pocketbook. But this
approach is likely to be self-defeating. (Sorry about that.)
Unless business firms continue to build and improve their
plant and equipment, productivity will falter and the 3.3
percent growth rate in GNP will be one more unfulfilled

prophecy. The result would be a smaller-than-$19-billion annual growth dividend, thereby compounding our difficulties.

This leaves federal defense (6 percent of GNP) and consumer spending (64 percent) as the only candidates left for contraction. To realize a reordering of priorities, it all comes down to not *whether* to cut back on defense and/or consumer spending, but *how* and in what proportions. If national defense absorbs the entire decline, then consumer spending can remain unaffected. But national security requirements may prevent meaningful reductions in the defense budget, and then consumer spending will have to take the brunt of the squeeze. Given reordered priorities and reasonably full employment, every additional dollar spent on guns will mean a dollar less for butter (the old guns-and-butter problem that helped Paul Samuelson sell millions of copies of his textbook).

All of this suggests that consumer spending will indeed have to be curbed if we are to feed the Ugly Ducklings. This could be undertaken through a variety of governmental measures, including most prominently higher tax rates (don't laugh—pretty soon you may be paying your share) and selective credit controls. We look at both of these methods in the remainder of this chapter.

Reordered Priorities Mean Higher Taxes

The standard way to influence total consumer outlays is by varying tax rates—lowering them to encourage, and raising them to discourage, consumer spending. Higher tax rates thus emerge as the painful counterpart of reordered priorities. It is precisely here that the American public's desire for a true reordering of priorities meets its severest test, because any significant restraint on consumer spending must necessarily imply higher taxes on middle-income families. As a practical matter, reduced consumption simply cannot be accomplished primarily by increasing taxes on business or the wealthy.

Higher business taxes are likely to inhibit investment rather than consumer spending. But business investment in new plant and equipment, as emphasized above, is needed for an adequate growth rate. Despite recent questioning of some of the by-products of economic growth, the fact remains that it is still the most important single generator of usable resources.

"Soaking the rich" is no answer either. Raising taxes on the rich, say on those with annual incomes over $100,000, might be justifiable on grounds of equity but it is not likely to go far toward the objective of reducing consumer spending. The rich do not account for that much consumer spending in the first place, and of all taxpayers they would be the most likely to react to higher taxes by cutting back their saving rather than their spending. Nor, of course, can any help be expected from reducing the consumption of those already at or close to the subsistence level.

The conclusion is inescapable: A large share of the cost of reordered priorities (less consumption) will have to be borne (in taxes) by middle-income families; it is they who comprise the bulk of the population and who do most of the consumer spending.

An alternative to explicitly higher tax rates is the *implicit* tax imposed through inflation. Increased spending on the Ugly Ducklings, without reductions in either defense or consumer spending, is likely to strain the economy's productive capacity and drive prices higher. The result generally is to contract most the consumption of those least able to protect themselves, such as the elderly and others living on fixed incomes and fringe workers in nonunionized employment.

Finally, there is the direct attack on poverty per se. This is somewhat different from the kinds of things we have mentioned so far. Pollution control, upgrading the quality of education, and so forth, involve the shifting of resources from one category of spending to another. The objective of income maintenance programs, on the other hand, is not to direct spending to particular uses, but to direct income to particular persons; the main effect would be a redistribution within the total of consumer spending, from upper income groups toward lower.

It has been estimated by the Census Bureau that direct action to bring all Americans up to the subsistence level, via some plan of family allowances or negative income taxes, would cost more than $15 billion a year. Again, this would have to be financed in substantial part by taxes on middle-income families, because that is where most of the income is.

Can Selective Credit Controls Help?

Taxes hurt. You have to dig into your pocket—aggravating your tennis elbow. They may also inhibit work incentives, as we saw in chapter 13, reducing aggregate production and economic well-being. Politicians, long aware of the unpopularity of higher taxes, have sought a less painful way to reorder national priorities.

Selective credit policies are the politicians' favorite alternative to taxation in reallocating resources among different uses. Such policies include prohibitory regulations regarding certain uses of credit, such as consumer credit and real estate credit controls; favored legal status to lenders who make certain types of loans, such as the favorable tax treatment received by savings and loan associations as a quid pro quo for their concentrating on mortgage lending and the line of credit at the Treasury granted to the Federal National Mortgage Association in exchange for operating a secondary market in mortgages; and interest rate subsidies to certain categories of borrowers for making particular kinds of expenditures, such as students who are borrowing from banks to finance their education and poor families who are taking out mortgages to finance the purchase of homes.

This list only scratches the surface of the myriad of selective credit policies currently on the books in the United States. At last count, there were over fifty general categories of federal credit programs in operation, and that count did not include either the usury laws or the regulations imposed on financial institutions to channel credit into particular uses, such as the portfolio restrictions on savings and loan associations and the various legal lending limits imposed on commercial banks.

New selective credit policies are, in fact, being proposed all the time. For example, Andrew Brimmer, a former member of the Board of Governors of the Federal Reserve System, has suggested that banks be required to have different reserve ratios on various categories of loans—higher ratios to discourage unfavored types of loans and lower ratios to encourage favored types.

At this point it is appropriate to ask at least four questions:

(1) How are selective credit policies supposed to work? (2) Do they in fact work successfully? (3) What's wrong with them? (4) Why are they so popular?

A Catechism on Selective Credit Policies

QUESTION: *How are selective credit policies supposed to work?*

ANSWER: Their objective is to encourage (or discourage) a particular type of real expenditure—say, housing or consumer durable goods expenditures—by increasing (or decreasing) the volume of credit directed to such activities and/or by making the terms of credit (interest rates, downpayments) easier or more stringent. One obvious prerequisite for the effectiveness of selective credit policies is that there be a close relationship between a specific type of credit and a particular category of real expenditure. For example, as long as the purchase of a home is closely related to the availability of mortgage credit, it is possible to encourage housing by inducing lenders to make mortgage loans rather than other types of loans. As lenders devote more funds to mortgages and less, say, to business loans, the interest rate on mortgages should fall in relation to the rate on business loans, and people will thus be encouraged to take out mortgages and buy new homes.

But that is not the only way to use mortgage money. What if someone already has enough cash to buy a home and is ready to spend it for that purpose regardless of mortgage terms? The availability of cheap mortgage money then induces him to take out a mortgage to finance his home—

freeing his other funds for more serious endeavors, like a six-month tour of the world's sunniest beaches.

A selective credit policy will be most effective in redirecting real resources when there is a rigid dollar-for-dollar relationship between a specific type of credit and a particular category of expenditure. To the extent that there is some slippage—that is, as long as the expenditure can be financed in other ways or the specific type of credit can be used differently—the effectiveness of the selective credit policy is impaired.

Many selective credit policies are imposed on only one sector of the financial markets, such as Brimmer's proposal that commercial banks have different reserve requirements on different types of loans. Such selective credit policies increase the flow of credit to the favored uses only so long as other (unrestricted) lenders in financial markets do not counteract their behavior. For instance, if Brimmer's proposal were enacted and the reserve requirement against mortgage loans were low while the reserve requirement against consumer installment loans were high, banks would find it profitable to divert more funds to mortgages and less to consumer installment credit. Initially, mortgage rates would decline and consumer credit rates would go up. This is precisely the desired objective of the selective credit policy. *But* the reaction of other institutional lenders, such as life insurance companies, might then be to make fewer mortgage loans and to expand credit to consumer installment loans, which will ultimately tend to offset the impact of the selective policy. As long as this offset is incomplete, however, selective credit policies on only a few sectors of the credit market can successfully divert some funds into favored uses.

QUESTION: *Do they in fact work successfully?*

ANSWER: Under most circumstances, selective credit policies do seem to work. Imposing regulations and controls does appear to succeed in diverting credit into desired channels. Furthermore, borrowers do tend, for the most part, to use certain types of credit for specific types of real expenditures. However, the very success of selective credit controls is likely to sow the seeds of their ultimate failure. If consumers cannot get credit from banks to finance the purchase of automobiles because, say, the banks are preoccupied with sewage bonds of local municipalities, then the auto dealers will arrange the necessary financing. How? Most probably through the auto manufacturers, who can float bonds in the capital markets and use the proceeds for anything they want, including extending loans to potential customers.

QUESTION: *What's wrong with selective credit policies?*

ANSWER: For one thing, as indicated in the preceding paragraph, their effectiveness tends to wear out with the passage of time. Another drawback is that the real costs of such programs are obscured by the financial maze. The unavoidable fact of life is that there is no such thing as a free lunch—when we are already close to full employment, the cost of more resources in education or housing has to be fewer resources available for other things. This lesson is brought home loud and clear when taxes must be raised to deter the other types of expenditure, with the proceeds going to the favored groups.

But favoring some borrowers (and thereby in effect squeezing others out of the credit market), while less direct than taxation, has similar social costs—less of something else. If politicians are not aware of these costs (and the proliferation of credit programs makes it doubtful that they are), then the indiscriminate use of selective credit policies tries to favor everyone and everything and winds up producing nothing.

QUESTION: *Why are selective credit policies so popular?*

ANSWER: Partly because they don't *seem* to be as painful as taxation. Those who are unable to buy new cars because they can't get financing are likely to blame fate or the world in general, while those who can't buy them because they have so little left after taxes are likely to blame the politicians in power. Also, more positively, selective credit policies do have the attractive feature of making the private sector an active partner in the process of redirecting resources. The government only provides the incentive—an interest subsidy, insurance for the lender against default, or some other feature. The bulk of the funds are still channeled through nongovernmental institutions.

The scope of activities currently receiving favorable treatment in the credit markets extends from exports and foreign economic development to community redevelopment and higher education. Housing, however, stands head-and-shoulders above all other activities as the spending category receiving the most credit favors. Unfortunately, it is impossible to judge whether the benefits of these programs exceed the costs they impose. And that, in itself, is cause for serious concern.

18

EQUAL OPPORTUNITY IN BANKING:

THE CASE FOR AND AGAINST

JOB QUOTAS

In recent years, equal employment opportunity for women and minorities has become a declared objective of national economic policy. How can we best provide such equal job opportunity in banking, as well as elsewhere? One view is that job quotas would be a useful instrument toward this end, but this position is challenged by others who believe just as firmly that quotas would be more harmful than helpful.

Indicative of current polarization on this issue, the authors of this book hold opposite opinions on the subject of quotas. While we have been able to reconcile our differences on everything else, when it comes to quotas we find ourselves unable to agree. So in this chapter only, we have to present our views separately. After reading both sides, you can come to your own conclusion (as you should on everything, anyway).

I. THE CASE FOR JOB QUOTAS (RITTER)

Job quotas have been advocated as a means of boring through the encrusted prejudice that, long after passage of the 1964 Civil Rights Act, still restricts employment opportunities for women and minorities. To get their "fair share" of jobs, proponents want quotas established, requiring that women and minorities be employed in virtually all occupations and at virtually all levels in rough proportion to their percentage distribution in the local labor force.

In reaction, angry opposition has arisen from employers, unions, ethnic groups, and religious organizations, almost irrespective of their "liberal" or "conservative" views on other issues. They maintain that hiring should be based solely on individual qualifications, that promotion should depend strictly on individual merit, without regard to a person's race, color, sex, religion, or national origin. Indeed, in executive suites and union halls, job quotas are usually considered a subject fit only for ridicule ("How about a quota in professional basketball for people less than six feet tall?").

Who is right? Are job quotas based on race or sex more likely to enhance equality of opportunity or destroy it?

Employment Patterns in Banking

The pattern of minority and female employment in the banking industry has been so widely publicized in recent years, that a brief recapitulation of some of the major findings is sufficient.

On the basis of 1966 data, Governor Andrew Brimmer of the Federal Reserve Board reported that only 4 percent of the jobs in banking were held by blacks, although they comprise about 10 percent of the population. In addition, one-third of those blacks who did work in banks were concentrated in the service workers category (janitors, and so on), even though service worker jobs are but a small fraction (5 percent) of total employment in banks. Further, among those blacks who were in white-collar bank jobs, almost none were at the professional or managerial level, although a fifth of all white-collar bank jobs fall into that classification. With respect to women, the pattern was somewhat different: almost all were white-collar workers, but hardly any above the office and clerical worker level (whereas half of the male white-collar workers in banks were in professional and managerial positions).

A later investigation (1971) by the Council on Economic Priorities revealed some improvement since the mid-1960s, but not enough to make more than a marginal change in the basic picture. Minorities were still concentrated disproportionately in service and clerical jobs, women still in clerical jobs. Relatively few of either were in professional or managerial positions (although more women are executives in banking than in any other industry).

Data for 1974 showed that minorities represented 16 percent of the work force in banks but had only 5 percent of the professional or managerial positions. Women made up two-thirds of the work force in banks but had only one-fifth of the higher-ranking jobs. There appears to have been some progress in the late seventies and the early eighties, especially in the larger banks in the larger cities, but there is still a long way to go before we reach true equal employment opportunity for all.

Unfair Demand or Unqualified Supply?

By itself, the fact that minorities and women are concentrated disproportionately in lower-echelon bank jobs, if they are employed at all, does not prove that banks discriminate unfairly against them—just as the difficulties small business-men have in getting bank loans when money is tight do not prove unfair bank discrimination against them. Banks give priority to their most creditworthy customers; since small businesses are more prone to default than larger ones, when funds become scarce small firms are likely to feel the pinch most. The pattern of employment in banking may similarly reflect, at least in part, a scarcity of women and minorities *qualified* to perform managerial or executive functions.

In other words, the present composition of employment in banking may be due to supply shortages as much as or more than demand biases. A similar argument has been made by many universities—they claim that try as they might they simply cannot find many female or minority group Ph.D.s to staff their faculties. Observation does confirm that banks and colleges seeking qualified women or minorities for higher-echelon positions have frequently encountered supply short-ages, particularly in the past few years.

Why should this be? One does not have to look far, of course, to find the answer. Blacks and Puerto Ricans, to take two glaring examples, generally grow up in slum neighbor-hoods, go to grossly inferior schools, encounter majority group hostility at an early age, and learn in countless ways that the cards are stacked against them. In such an environ-ment, childhood and adolescence involve not growing up but being ground down.

With respect to bank employment, two levels of discrimi-nation are therefore relevant. One is job discrimination, prej-udiced demand; the other is general environmental discrimi-nation, ultimately responsible for shortages of qualified supply. Even if every bank in the country suddenly were to become an equal opportunity employer in fact as well as name, this would have little bearing on general environmental discrimination inflicted on minorities *before* they ever enter the job market. Given the prevalence of environmental discrimination, it is hardly surprising that a sudden reduction in job discrimination should find comparatively few minority group members ready for careers in banking.

It is not particularly fruitful to try to unravel which is more responsible for the present employment profile in banking—job discrimination that shrinks the demand for women and minorities, or general environmental discrimination that eventually shows up in the guise of unqualified supply—since it is necessary to reduce discrimination at both levels before significant improvement can occur in the composition of bank employment. Less job discrimination alone will lead only to unfillable demands for women and minorities, and less environmental discrimination alone will lead only to more college-educated typists and tellers.

The conclusion is obvious: A *multipronged* antidiscrimination program is necessary. Not so obvious is the key role, within this context, that job quotas can play.

Public Policy: Rhetoric or Numbers?

Governmental measures intended to expand equal employment opportunity include: (1) general rights legislation; (2) a variety of special-purpose manpower training programs (Neighborhood Youth Corps, Job Corps, New Careers); and (3) promotion of "affirmative action" programs, setting forth "goals" and "timetables" for hiring and advancing women and minorities.

At first, opposition to "affirmative action" was neither more nor less vocal than opposition to any proposed remedy for discriminatory employment practices. Antagonism escalated, however, as soon as government officials, under pressure from minority groups, suggested that employers and unions move beyond general goals and actually specify the *number* of women and minorities they planned to admit at various levels over a scheduled time period. The reaction was vehement. The *New York Times,* for example, speaking for many who had previously approved of "affirmative action" programs, warned of "the danger of turning the government's fair employment goals and timetables into covert quotas," and commended those government officials who had shown awareness of the "peril" (editorial, October 12, 1972).

General goals, in the form of "good faith and effort," evidently meet with widespread approval. But when the goals are made more specific, their content concrete in the form of numbers, then approval rapidly shifts to opposition. Any numerical employment goal can always be expressed as a quota, and vice versa—that is, an employment objective can be expressed in terms of so many workers (a goal) or in terms of a certain percentage of a company's work force (a quota).

Thus, when quotas are denounced, what is really being condemned is the evolution of a *general* goal into a *quantitative* one. Since it is difficult to implement, enforce, or even evaluate a goal until it is quantified, apparently "affirmative action" programs are acceptable to many when they affirm but not when they act.

Fortunately, the United States Supreme Court has taken a meaningful stand in favor of action as well as affirmation. The landmark 1978 *Bakke* decision, for example, permits colleges and universities to treat race and minority status as a positive factor in the admissions process. Colleges and universities can not establish "quotas" or guarantee a specific number of places for minority students and women, but they can set "numerical goals" in rough and general terms. Similarly, the 1979 *Weber* decision upheld affirmative action programs designed to correct past discriminatory practices as manifest in racial imbalances in employment, and the 1980 *Fullilove* v. *Klutznick* decision explicitly endorsed the power of Congress to take racial status into account in awarding federal contracts.

Opposition to job quotas and quantitative goals can be classified under three headings:

1. You Can't Fight Human Nature—the objective of equal employment opportunity is misguided.

2. The Private Sector Can Take Care of It—the objective is worthy, but it lies outside the legitimate scope of governmental intervention.

3. You're on the Right Track But the Wrong Road—the objective is worthy, and government intervention to achieve it is desirable, but job quotas and numerical goals are not the proper means to use.

You Can't Fight Human Nature

To many, the whole idea of equal employment is misguided. By virtue of thousands of years of Darwinian natural selection, combined with the blessings of free enterprise, employment and responsibility already are distributed in accordance with talent and ability. The people on top are there because they can do the job, and those in the middle and on the bottom are there because that's where they belong. Men are men and women are women. Whites are white and blacks are black, and Puerto Ricans and Chicanos shouldn't be here to begin with. If people would only learn their place and do their job properly, we'd all be better off.

It is difficult to argue logically against this position. In effect, it speaks for itself.

The Private Sector Can Take Care of It

To others, the objective of equal employment opportunity is worthy, but it lies outside the legitimate scope of governmental intervention. The problem, it is said, can best be resolved by leaving it to the initiative of the private sector. But the private sector, left to its own devices, has not eliminated discrimination. And in this day and age, it is difficult to imagine any general principle that would bar the government from the pursuit of equal employment opportunity, while at the same time permitting the present scope and depth of government involvement elsewhere in the economy.

In fact, federally supervised job quotas would do no more than combine three well-established areas of federal activity. Government actions directed toward employment in general have been well accepted since the Employment Act of 1946, as have government activities regarding discrimination in general since the Civil Rights Act of 1964 (not to mention the Fourteenth Amendment of 1868). And government quota-setting is nothing new either—witness crude oil import quotas, farm acreage allotment quotas, and immigration quotas, to name but three.

The Federal Reserve Act itself contains not one, but two quotas. With respect to the Board of Directors of each Federal Reserve Bank, directors by statute specifically represent banking interests, commercial interests, and the general public. With respect to the Board of Governors in Washington, membership is limited to no more than one governor from a Federal Reserve District, and the Board's composition must also reflect "fair representation" of the country's financial, agricultural, commercial, and industrial interests.

You're on the Right Track but the Wrong Road

More typical of objections to job quotas and numerical goals is the widely held view that while the objective of equal employment opportunity is worth pursuing, and governmental intervention to achieve it desirable, nevertheless these are not the proper means to use: hiring and promotion should *always* be determined by individual merit, *never* on the basis of racial, religious, sexual, or nationality criteria. Governmental antidiscrimination measures should be confined to general civil rights legislation, manpower training programs, and the like.

At the outset, a distinction should be drawn between means and ends, between the methods used to achieve objectives and the objectives themselves. And it should be made clear that proponents of job quotas *also* seek hiring and promotion based on individual merit. The real dispute is, therefore, not about objectives, but about the most effective means of reaching them. Can equal job opportunity, based on individual ability, be more realistically attained with or without the use of quotas? Opponents of numerical goals argue that their very use subverts equal opportunity, by substituting racial, sexual, or nationality criteria in place of individual merit.

In more general terms, the issue is whether *any* ultimate objective can ever be achieved through means that apparently contradict it. In such general terms, without specific reference to employment, it should be clear that ultimate objectives indeed *are* frequently realized via methods that on the surface appear contradictory. Men fight to preserve peace, surgeons amputate to maintain life, families consume less (this year) to consume more (next year), and banks sacrifice earnings (in the short run) to increase earnings (in the long run). Sometimes it works and sometimes it doesn't. In the final analysis, each individual case can only be decided on the basis of its unique circumstances.

The Merits of Quotas

With specific reference to equal employment opportunity as an objective, the merits of job quotas and quantitative goals as a means toward that end are more persuasive than generally realized:

1. It is popular to be for job "goals" for minorities and women, and against "quotas." But, as noted, a quota is nothing more than a quantitative goal. Only by attaching numbers to a goal can it be assessed as to its reasonableness, implemented according to a time schedule, evaluated on the basis of performance, and enforced objectively. In practical terms, the only goals that are operational—in contrast to rhetorical—are quantitative ones.

2. The main reason for proposing job quotas—requiring that women and minorities be employed, in virtually all occupations and at virtually all levels, in rough proportion to their percentage distribution in the local labor force—is not to start the use of racial, sexual, or nationality criteria in employment, but to stop it. Job quotas are not advocated in a vacuum. They are advocated as an antidote to the widespread implicit quotas that already exist, quotas that already employ racial, religious, and sexual criteria, but use them *against* minorities and women.

Proposed quotas are typically judged by comparing them with ideal conditions, wherein everyone is hired and promoted strictly on the basis of individual merit. But such a comparison is misleading; in the real world at the present time those ideal conditions simply do not exist. The realistic comparison is between the informal, quietly administered quotas that currently protect entrenched privilege and restrict opportunity; and formal, mutually established, and government-enforced quotas that would break down such barriers and expand opportunity. To be against opportunity-expanding quotas today because one has been opposed to opportunity-restricting quotas in the past is like taking a stand against the scalpel because one is opposed to the dagger.

3. It is frequently argued that quotas will reduce effi-

ciency and thereby raise costs. It is not immediately apparent, however, why job quotas should be any more efficiency-inhibiting than many other widely accepted employment practices, such as, for example, seniority in the factory and tenure in the classroom, both of which involve employment criteria other than individual ability. Seniority in the factory favors longtime employees, although newer ones may be more productive; tenure in the university protects the jobs of older professors, although younger ones may be better teachers and more capable scholars. Why is it that seniority and tenure are not opposed with the same intensity as employment goals for minorities and women?

4. Job quotas are no panacea. They cannot do the job alone. They are obviously most directly applicable in counteracting job discrimination (prejudiced demand). But their effectiveness is minimized without a corresponding diminution in general environmental discrimination, to expand the supply of qualified women and minorities.

General environmental discrimination is not directly susceptible to treatment by job quotas. More relevant are other governmental policies that would meaningfully upgrade the quality and quantity of low-income housing, radically improve inner city public school systems, expand federally sponsored job training programs, and so on. Even here, however, job quotas have indirect implications: once established, they would put many who have traditionally lobbied against such programs in a position where, for the first time, they have a financial stake in their success. If hiring and promotion were quota-influenced, for example, business firms would be more directly concerned with the quality of ghetto schools. And if blacks and other minorities were not such a disproportionate percentage of the unemployed, public policies to reduce both aggregate and structural unemployment would probably be more vigorously pursued.

Put somewhat differently, as matters stand the costs of both job discrimination and general environmental discrimination are now borne entirely by those who are discriminated against. Job quotas would force a more equal sharing of those costs among the population as a whole. The more widely the costs are distributed, the more likely that the political process will generate real pressures to eliminate the underlying discrimination.

5. In summary, the main reason for imposing job quotas is the prevalence of already existing discriminatory practices. The ultimate objective of quotas is equality of employment opportunity, elimination of discrimination, and thus their own demise. When there is no more discrimination, there will be no more need for quotas.

Quotas per se are neither good nor bad, any more than nuclear energy, drugs, or money can be said, per se, to be good or bad. Some quotas restrict opportunity and some expand it. Even among those that expand it, the desirability of any particular quota system cannot be evaluated in the abstract. It depends, in each instance, on the reasons for establishing it; the alternatives to it; its applicability to the particular type of job, occupation, or profession; and its specific provisions, including the time schedule set for its targets to be reached. These are the concrete issues that deserve serious consideration, within realistic contexts, not whether quotas in the abstract are "right" or "wrong." It would be ironic if such matters continue to be dismissed out of hand by invocation of the very ideal that they could help make a reality: hiring and promotion based, in fact as well as principle, on individual merit—regardless of race, color, sex, religion, or national origin.

II. DON'T DO IT WITH QUOTAS (SILBER)

There are good quotas and bad quotas—good for me and bad for you; good for banking, but bad for basketball; good for financial institutions, bad for football. To those advocating quotas to redress imbalances in the employment of "minority groups" in banking and financial institutions, I respond with an equally disturbing proposal: quotas to rectify imbalances in the employment of "minority groups" in football or basketball. The minority groups are quite different in each case and are necessarily defined within a very specific context. Blacks and women (at 51 percent of the population, obviously not a real minority) are the *relevant* minority groups as far as the business world is concerned, while in the sports world the underprivileged are skinny kids with glasses.

That is a ridiculous analogy. Everyone knows that basketball demands certain skills. Requiring 25 percent (or whatever the relevant number is) of all professional basketball players to have such *irrelevant* characteristics is certain to do at least three things: destroy the incentive of some to invest their own time, money, and effort to develop the requisite basketball skills; penalize those who have already done so; and lower the quality of the product that is offered the public.

Most quotas are bad—they introduce the same type of distortions and inequities as the ones just ridiculed. And yet, there are "good" quotas of which we are very proud—one man, one vote; equal radio and TV time for candidates to public office; 100 percent of all children under sixteen must be in school. And there are quotas that are quite necessary —100 percent of those without driver's licenses cannot sit behind the steering wheel. Quotas that set a floor, a minimum percentage, for minority employment in banking or any other industry do not fall into the category of either proud quotas or necessary quotas. They are bad quotas that must be resisted in favor of other means of redressing the evils of any type of discrimination.

The Need for Government Intervention

The rationale of a free market economy, as opposed to one that is centrally planned, rests on the foundation that the decisions of what to produce, how, and for whom, are best made within a competitive environment, with each individual free to decide based on the information received from the price system. This is not the place to go into the elegant proofs of efficiency of the price system. Let us assume it is so, just as we can also assume that discrimination by sex, race, or religion is bad, and that it exists.

There are situations, of course, when the price system is faulty, and here government intervention is called for. The price system, for example, rewards each individual according to the quality of his or her own performance. But what if my actions also benefit others? If I educate myself, I benefit because of increased future earnings, but others benefit because I am literate and because I behave more civilly (presumably). The solution—encourage literacy and civics via free public education. Similarly, if my actions injure others, the price system is also modified. I may be able to afford a car—but if I drive it without knowing how, others may be killed. The solution—the motor vehicles bureau and licensing.

Another type of intervention comes in the form of "it's good for you even though you don't know it." In general, consumers buy what they like, and that's why the price they are willing to pay is a good measure of the value of the product. But under some conditions the government suspends the price system to "give us what is good for us" (can we ever get too much of a good thing?)—free milk to schoolchildren rather than a quarter to buy whatever they like.

In some areas the price system is eliminated completely. In politics, unlike economics, the quota is one man, one vote, not one dollar, one vote. The price system has been eliminated because of philosophical and ethical principles inherent in the democratic form of government.

Finally, the government intervenes when free competition is prevented from operating: when prices don't reflect consumers' desires—they are set by monopolists; or when an individual is not rewarded according to performance (or is denied access to the requisite education or training)—because of artificial barriers to entry.

This last category justifies government intervention in the form of antitrust legislation and antidiscrimination laws. Quotas for minority employment must be justified in this context if they are to be accepted as a legitimate form of government interference with the market.

There is surely no philosophical or ethical principle that would *require* women or blacks to make up 27.3 or 42.6 percent of middle management positions in banking; there is only the principle that they have the opportunity to do so.

Equality of opportunity is the watchword, not equality of result. Similarly, while there might be benefits to some if women or blacks make up a minimum portion of the banking industry, there are others who might be hurt. Discrimination by race, sex, or religion must be eliminated, but the use of minority employment quotas is just a means toward achieving that goal, certainly not an end in itself. It must be justified as the best means toward that end, or fall by the wayside in favor of some other mechanism for setting things right.

The Economics of Quotas

It would be hard to find an economist who prefers the long-run results of minimum employment quotas to an effectively implemented set of antidiscrimination laws. The solution to monopoly power is to break it up via antitrust legislation, not to give other firms similar market strength. The analogy to discrimination in employment is perfect; the solution is effective implementation of antidiscrimination laws and not perpetuating the discrimination ethos by quotas for each section of the population. In the extreme, that solution approaches the most abhorrent of them all—the caste system in India.

Quotas are more popular among noneconomists, especially politicians, or politically-minded economists. The reasons are not hard to find. Quotas seem to be a quick way to achieve the objective of equal employment treatment of races, ethnics, and sexes. They also are beloved by politicians because they don't cost anything in federal or state budgets; they don't create the need for taxes. One doesn't have to be from Missouri to be suspicious of quick solutions that don't have any apparent costs. And in this case the doubts are well founded.

Quotas impose real costs on society which are very difficult to measure but are there nevertheless. One serious drawback, therefore, of minimum employment quotas compared with other antidiscrimination tools is that we cannot measure their real cost. An intelligent government program must be evaluated in terms of costs versus benefits. When taxes are imposed to implement a program, they are a straightforward measure of costs. When they are compared with the benefits of the program, it is possible to decide if people are better off without (both the taxes and the program). Not so with quotas.

Minimum employment quotas impose at least two categories of costs. First, there is the direct cost to a bank of training less qualified applicants for a job. The barriers to entry that create the problems of discrimination in employment stem, in part, from inferior educations provided by ghetto schools and by the social mores characteristic of our society. While there still may be many who are merely "standing at the gates waiting to get in," a significant problem involves removing the legacy of discrimination that began further back in the chain. Retraining, reeducating, and rehabilitating (the three R's) the relevant minority groups is certainly a cost that will be incurred. There is no reason for such costs, stemming largely from the failure of society as a whole, to be borne by individual banks or other firms.

But even if individual banks are at fault (because they set up artificial barriers) and are willing to redress the legacy of discrimination and absorb the cost of the three R's, there is an even more significant, if less obvious, set of costs imposed by quotas. Those who have already invested time, money, and effort to acquire the requisite training and skills will be deprived of their expected returns by administrative fiat.

Furthermore, incentives that are a crucial component of a free market economy, insuring that resources are used in the best possible way, will be destroyed. A bank may appear magnanimous in its willingness to absorb the costs of breaking down discriminatory practices. But in reality, it is absorbing only a small fraction of the costs; it shifts the remainder onto society as a whole (reduced incentives), and it also burdens innocent bystanders with the pecuniary and nonpecuniary costs of having prepared themselves for a productive role in the economy, only to be denied access under the rubric of justice to others.

One can certainly argue that a bank in violation of antidiscrimination laws should be fined, and rather severely (treble damages?). But the question of who should bear the full costs of removing discrimination by race, sex, or religion is quite another matter. A clear case can be made for society as a whole, since discrimination and unequal opportunity are perpetrated by many institutions and at different stages. That suggests distributing the costs via the best vehicle governments have yet devised—taxation. Joseph Pechman, a tax expert from the Brookings Institution, emphasizes that the objective of any tax system is to distribute the cost of government fairly; whatever the shortcomings of the tax system, there is no better way for us to proceed.

A less popular case can be made for the group that benefits most to bear the costs of removing discrimination. While collective action is necessary to remove discriminatory practices, those who are the objects of discrimination stand to gain most from their removal, hence they should bear the greatest portion of the costs. This suggests self-help organizations, lobbying groups, economic boycotts, and so on, in order to force society to eliminate discrimination. The cost of change in such instances is borne primarily by the minorities, not by society, and there is sufficient precedent for such self-help groups organized by many different minorities in their fight for equal rights.

None of the arguments suggests that the costs ought to be imposed on those who have already invested time, money, and effort in acquiring skills. Nor do they suggest that the costs should come in the form of reduced incentives. In fact, the optimum type of government intervention in such matters comes when individual incentives are left unimpaired. *There is a reasonable case for using the tax system to distribute the costs, and a less reasonable case for using the benefit principle, but there is no case at all for using a haphazard, inequitable, and inefficient mechanism such as quotas.*

The Political Economy of Quotas

Alexander Hamilton, the first secretary of the Treasury, unwittingly made the best case for minimum employment quotas for minorities. In particular, he argued for tariffs or quotas on foreign goods in order to protect "infant industries" in the young American economy. While interference with free trade via tariffs causes inefficiencies, it may be justified in order to permit an industry to get started; once started, it will be able to hold its own without protection. The tariff is just a temporary measure which will be suspended when the industry grows up. Similarly, minimum employment quotas, so the argument goes, are a temporary means for getting minorities started in heretofore "foreign" occupations. Once the barrier is broken, quotas will be removed and minorities will fend for themselves.

Paul Samuelson provided the best commentary on protecting infant industries via tariffs or quotas: history reveals that most such cases produce perpetual infants. Once imposed, quotas are almost impossible to remove; while they are justified as *short-run solutions* they are transformed, via political realities, into *long-run institutions.*

Quota-lovers simply cannot be taken seriously when the minimum employment quotas for minorities are put forth as a temporary means to achieve the lofty goal of nondiscrimination by race and sex. In fact, it is paradoxical that quotas should be used in this context, since that is the very thing we are trying to root out. They are proposing minimum quotas to destroy maximum quotas (no blacks or women). Aside from the reasonable proposition that minimum employment quotas should be just as illegal as maximum quotas (anyone living in an apartment house readily recognizes that one person's floor is someone else's ceiling), they also perpetuate the race and sex differences they seek to overcome. As long as there are other means to achieve the objective, one need not adopt methods of dubious morality.

The Right Way

What means should be used to redress the evils of discrimination? The best solution is vigorous enforcement of the antidiscrimination laws in education and employment. Great strides have already been made in this regard. As far back as 1971, Governor Andrew Brimmer of the Federal Reserve Board presented a study to the NAACP and said, "it is also clear from the above analysis that blacks who are well-prepared to compete for higher paying positions in the upper reaches of the occupation structure have made measurable gains." Brimmer goes on to cite increased employment percentages to indicate special progress in communications, banking, and insurance. While Brimmer's data have not been updated, there is good reason to believe that similar gains continued through the 1970s.

As an aside, it should be noted that employment percentage numbers should be used with great reservation. They contain serious limitations in proving or revealing anything about discrimination. There is little reason to expect each ethnic group to be represented proportionately in all occupations. While intelligence may be normally distributed in the population, we do not, cannot, and should not assume that occupational choice is unaffected by family background and social interrelationships.

We can certainly do more in implementing antidiscrimination statutes. But it must be done on an individual, case-by-case basis. The speed with which individual violations are heard and adjudicated is of great importance. Government funds must be spent to set up "human rights commissions" and to streamline hearings of individual cases. The existence of quick access to the courts, accompanied by stiff pecuniary penalties to those found guilty, will help employers and others recognize the futility and potential costs of setting up artificial barriers.

Efficient and effective judicial review is not costless. Indeed, one of the advantages of this mechanism is that we know what it costs. It has none of the drawbacks of quotas and it militates against their perpetuation.

A case might also be made, not only to destroy discriminatory practices, but to help *all* those at the poverty level to overcome their lack of skills so that they can become more productive members in the economy. Manpower retraining programs, subsidies, or tax credits to employers who retrain those who are unemployed or those whose incomes are below a certain level can be instituted. But care must be taken *not* to tie eligibility to race, sex, or ethnic background. Information about such programs should be distributed widely and frequently, not only to black ghettos, but to all potential participants. Despite the stereotyped notions of who is poor, they aren't all, or even mostly, black. The others deserve as much or as little retraining and preferential treatment as the minorities currently in the public eye.

Knowing how much the antipoverty-discrimination programs cost in terms of foregone tax revenues (in the case of tax credits) and/or increased budget expenditures is a prerequisite for intelligent government intervention. We then can tell how much we are willing to give up for such matters. We are also able to distribute the costs equitably, via taxation. *Quotas sweep the costs out of sight, but not out of society.* Quotas appear to have the advantage of producing quick results, but they may not be much faster than an appropriate level of budget expenditure or tax relief. Every proponent of quotas submits a timetable, knowing full well that the shorter the horizon the greater the distortions and inequities. The types of programs listed here can match that timetable with an appropriate level of expenditure, only now we'll know what it really costs.

However appealing to those clamoring for action, quotas in banking and in every other industry hide the true costs, create inequities in the process, cause short-run and long-run misallocations compared with other solutions—and may not be any quicker in achieving the goal of equal employment opportunity.

PART VII

International Finance

19

MONEY IN INTERNATIONAL

FINANCE

The United States has had a deficit in its international balance of payments almost every year since 1949, which, as everyone knows, is a Bad Thing. As a result we have lost more than half of our gold, and *this,* it goes without saying, is an even more Serious Matter. We were the proud owners of 700 million ounces of gold in 1949, and now we have only about 260 million ounces left.

What to do?

An international "balance of payments" is an accounting record of all payments made across national borders. For each country it shows the payments made to foreigners and the receipt of funds from them, in the same way that a family might keep a record of all its expenditures and receipts. Americans make payments to others, for example, when we import foreign goods, buy foreign securities, lend to other countries, build factories on the outskirts of London or in the suburbs of Rome, or travel abroad on our summer vacations. On the other side of the ledger, we take in money when foreigners pay us for our exports, buy our stocks or bonds, build television factories in Illinois, or visit the Grand Canyon.

A deficit in our balance of payments is no different from a deficit in a household's budget. It means that we have been paying out more money abroad than we have been taking in, possibly because we have been importing more than we have been exporting, or because more Americans are visiting Paris and London than foreign tourists are taking in the sights of Yonkers and Yazoo City. Foreigners thereby accumulate more dollars than they need for their payments to us, and in the ordinary course of events—at least prior to 15 August 1971—many of these dollars were presented to the United States Treasury with a polite but firm request that they be exchanged for gold. Until 15 August 1971 the Treasury stood ready to honor, promptly if not happily, all official foreign requests at the rate of one ounce of gold for every $35 tendered, but on that date President Nixon got tired of paying out so much gold and called the whole deal off.

A nation can hardly run balance of payments deficits forever (although the United States does seem determined to prove otherwise). Sooner or later, after all, a country has to pay for its imports, and to do that it has to get the money from somewhere—for example, by borrowing from abroad or by selling some of its own products to others (i.e., by exporting). To that end, a number of suggestions are constantly made to cure our chronic deficit—to stop paying out more than we take in. One remedy that has often been proposed by many in the international financial community, and occasionally echoed by some here at home, is old-fashioned discipline, otherwise known as the time-honored hickory stick treatment.

The Discipline of the Balance of Payments

Balance of payments disciplinarians believe that to spare the rod is to spoil the child. Their recommendations as to how we should go about restoring equilibrium in our international accounts are appropriately strict. The Federal Reserve should administer the hickory stick by contracting the money supply and raising interest rates until tight money succeeds in reducing GNP and lowering wages and prices. It is difficult to estimate how much unemployment this might involve—perhaps 15 or 20 percent of the labor force, at a minimum.

With a depression-level GNP, the incomes of Americans would be so low that we would be hard put to afford such "luxuries" as travel abroad and the purchase of so many foreign products. In addition, there would be effects stemming from the change in prices here relative to prices abroad. With lower costs and prices in the United States, foreign goods become relatively more expensive, which discourages Americans from buying so many Toyotas and transistor radios, thus reducing our imports. The lower price tags here would similarly encourage foreigners to buy more of our now cheaper goods and services, thereby expanding our exports. Less imports and more exports: we will be paying out less money abroad and taking in more, thus reducing and possibly eliminating our balance of payments deficit.

At the same time, it is expected that purely financial flows would reinforce these effects. The higher interest rates that tight money induces here would bring in some foreign money seeking our attractive-yielding securities, and domestic money that had formerly been invested in foreign securities would presumably now return home to buy bargain-priced American stocks and bonds.

This is called Defending the Dollar. Obviously it is not a pleasant process, involving as it does tight money to induce substantial unemployment—enough unemployment to wring lower wages and prices out of the economy—and a shrinking GNP. It is clear that it is based on the well-known Rocky Marciano Principle, that the best defense is a good offense: we defend the dollar by attacking the economy.

For those of you too young to remember, Rocky Marciano (Rocco Francis Marchegiano) was the world heavyweight boxing champion from September 1952 until he retired undefeated in April 1956. He never learned to box very well, but he didn't have to. He had forty-nine professional fights and won all of them, forty-three by knockouts.

Professor Marciano thus takes his place in the Annals of Economics, right behind Professor Phillips, of Phillips Curve fame (see chapter 6) and Professor E. J. Finagle, discoverer of Finagle's Law ("Inanimate objects are out to get us"). Of course, like all firm discipline, the Marciano Principle is administered reluctantly and only for our own good. Rest assured, it would hurt the Federal Reserve more than it would hurt the economy; the Federal Reserve said so itself when, on the basis of this sort of reasoning, it *raised* the discount rate from 1½ percent to 2½ percent on 9 October 1931 and then to 3½ percent on 16 October, a week later. (By 1931 the Great Depression was something more than a speck on the horizon; GNP had already fallen 25 percent below its 1929 level, and unemployment had already risen to over 15 percent of the labor force.)

The Gold Standard

The gold standard, which was in effect throughout much of the Western world during the last half of the 1800s and the first few decades of the 1900s, represented the Marciano Principle in action. What was the gold standard and how was it supposed to work?

Under the traditional gold standard, nations fixed the value of their money in terms of gold and stood ready to buy or sell gold freely at the established price. This necessarily resulted in a fixed exchange ratio of one nation's money in terms of another's, called the par (or parity) rate of exchange. Say the United States fixed $20 an ounce as the price of gold and Great Britain decided upon £5 an ounce: then the par rate of exchange would be $4 for £1, because both $4 and £1 could purchase equal amounts of gold.

This fixed rate of exchange was quite stable. It would not vary above or below par by more than the cost of shipping gold across the Atlantic. If an American importer of £100 worth of British goods (woolen underwear) found that he was being charged more than $400 plus gold shipping costs in order to get the £100 he needed to pay his supplier, he could always buy $400 worth of gold (20 ounces) from the U.S. Treasury and ship it to England at his own expense to discharge his obligation. Thus the price of a unit of foreign money could only rise to an upper limit, known as the gold export point, which was above the par of exchange by the amount of gold shipping costs.

Similarly, the price of foreign money could not fall below par by more than the cost of shipping gold. If an American exporter of $400 worth of snuff boxes to England found that he would be offered less than $400 minus gold shipping costs for the £100 he had coming, he could always simply request that 20 ounces of gold be shipped here at his expense. Thus the lower limit of the foreign exchange rate was called the gold import point.

Under the rules of the gold standard, the money supply of every nation was tied rigidly to its gold supply. The gold standard was then expected to be a self-equilibrating mechanism in which balance of payments deficits and surpluses were automatically corrected by flows of gold among nations. This gold flow mechanism was expected to work just like the hickory stick treatment. Say the United States had a deficit in its balance of payments because it had been importing more than it had been exporting. It would make up this deficit by shipping gold abroad. This would mean less gold here and more gold in Great Britain, which would decrease the money supply in the United States and increase the money supply in Great Britain. Tight money here and an enlarged money supply abroad would lead to lower prices and wages here and to higher prices and wages abroad. With lower prices and wages here relative to abroad, Americans would be discouraged from buying any more woolen underwear from England and the British would find our snuff boxes even better bargains than before. So our imports fall, our exports expand, and our balance of payments deficit is corrected. This is precisely the same as the Marciano Principle: We drive the domestic economy into recession in order to improve our international balance of payments!

This sacrifice of domestic stability on the altar of international stability led to the downfall of the gold standard in the early 1930s, and there is little likelihood that it will ever return. Nowadays, no nation is about to abdicate control over its domestic financial affairs in favor of gold or anything like it. Before the development of modern monetary and

fiscal policies, government intervention to influence the economy was unknown; because they knew no better, nations
suffered through depressions and inflations and simply
waited for times to improve. But it is not possible to turn
back the clock. It is an open question whether modern monetary-fiscal policies actually do more good than harm, but any
administration that failed to take strong action to alleviate
recessions and inflations—and tried to invoke gold as the
reason for its inaction—would hardly remain long in office.
Today monetary policy is expected to actively alter monetary
and credit conditions to influence domestic economic activity, not to passively adapt to changes in our gold stock
merely because it might restore equilibrium in our balance
of international payments.

Historically, a main function of the gold standard was to
serve as a safeguard against inflation, by tying the money
supply to gold and thereby providing an upper limit on the
money-issuing power of the state. Insofar as governments of
all sorts have a propensity to print excessive amounts of
money in order to finance wars and circuses, it was thought
that gold would play a useful role by forcing governments to
live within their means. No more gold, no more money.

However, in reality gold has usually proved to be extremely unreliable in preventing inflation. Even in the good
old days (remember them?), when coins were the sole circulating money, kings and princes found ways to circumvent
any gold shortage by clipping the coins (literally) and changing the rules. And today, with most of our money in the form
of checking accounts at various financial institutions and
with electronic money on the horizon, any conceivable connection between gold and the money supply is too tenuous
to rely on as an effective means of preventing excessive monetary expansion. The need to prevent inflation is undeniable,

but gold has never been dependable in that respect and is even less likely to be so today.

Nevertheless, one remnant of the gold standard did manage to hang on until 1973. At the end of World War II the nations of the world agreed to maintain fixed and inflexible exchange rates, more or less as under the gold standard. This led to periodic financial crises, as we shall see in the next chapter. Before turning to the performance of fixed exchange rates in the postwar period, however, let's examine another alternative: flexible (or floating) exchange rates.

Floating Exchange Rates

Another possible cure for a balance-of-payments deficit, one that does not clash so violently with the goals of high employment, stable prices, and economic growth, is to permit flexibility in the price of foreign money (or, what amounts to the same thing, in the foreign price of dollars). Say a Mexican peso costs Americans five cents and a French franc costs us twenty-five cents. Until early 1973, such prices of one kind of money in terms of another—or exchange rates—were rigidly fixed by international agreement under the overall supervision of the International Monetary Fund (IMF), an institution established at an international monetary conference held at Bretton Woods, New Hampshire, in 1944.

The IMF's main function was to oversee the stability of exchange rates, although it was really unable to prevent unilateral exchange rate alterations when nations individually decided it was in their self-interest to make such changes. From World War II until 1973 world monetary arrangements were based on a network of more or less fixed (or pegged) exchange rates, supervised by the IMF.

The alternative to a system of fixed exchange rates is to unpeg them, and let them float freely in accordance with supply and demand conditions for each particular country's money. An increase in the *supply* of Mexican pesos would lower their price, say from five cents to four cents a peso; an increase in the *demand* for French francs would raise their price, say from twenty-five cents to thirty cents a franc. This was not permitted under IMF monetary arrangements until 1973; actually, it wasn't *officially* permitted until 1976.

Remember that a deficit in our balance of payments means we are paying out more money abroad than we are taking in. American importers are paying out more dollars for Swiss cuckoo clocks and Scotch whisky than foreigners need to buy our exported Frisbees and Fords. Result: An excess supply of dollars (or an excess demand for foreign money, since you can look at it either way) builds up throughout the world.

When exchange rates are free to fluctuate in response to supply and demand, the excess supply of dollars—due to our spending so much abroad—depresses the price of dollars to foreigners. The dollar *depreciates* relative to other monies. (Instead of the French having to pay four francs to get a dollar, something *less* than four francs would get them that much of our money.)

Or you could look at the same thing from the other side of the transaction, in which case an excess supply of dollars translates into an excess demand for other monies. When we import toenail clippers from Hong Kong or hitchhike along the not-so-sunny coast of Portugal, we have to buy their money to make payments. You can either say we are supplying dollars or buying (demanding) foreign money. From the latter point of view, this excess demand for foreign money—

due to our spending so much abroad—raises the price of foreign money to Americans. Other monies *appreciate* relative to the dollar. (Instead of Americans getting a franc for twenty-five cents, we would have to pay *more* to get one franc.)

This depreciation of the dollar (or appreciation of other monies) has two effects. First, dollars become cheaper for foreigners, so our goods and services automatically become less expensive for them even though our domestic price tags remain unchanged. After all, it makes no difference to them whether our goods are less expensive for them because our price tags are lower (the Marciano method) or because each United States dollar costs them less of their own money while our price tags stay the same (the flexible exchange rate method). In either case our goods are cheaper for foreigners to buy, and our exports are likely to expand.

Second, foreign monies now cost us more, so that foreign goods and services automatically become more expensive for us to buy. With foreign products costing us more, because foreign money costs more, our purchases from abroad, our imports, are likely to fall.

Thus the end results are the same as the Marciano route: more exports and less imports. We take in more francs and pesos as we receive payment for our enlarged exports, and pay out less dollars abroad because of our lower imports, thereby putting an end to both the deficit in our balance of payments and the depreciation of the dollar. However, we achieve these results by letting exchange rates decline while keeping our economy stable, instead of by sending the economy into a nosedive while keeping exchange rates stable.

Freely floating exchange rates are a sharp departure from international monetary arrangements as they existed prior to

1973. Until then, fixed exchange rates, called par values, ruled the roost.

Most academic economists, both Monetarist and Keynesian, lean toward floating exchange rates. Most bankers and government officials, on the other hand, seem to favor a system of fixed exchange rates; they argue that freely floating rates create so much uncertainty regarding the price of foreign money that *international* trade is seriously impaired. Advocates of rate flexibility reply that fixed rates often create so much disruption at home—by forcing countries to adjust their economies instead of their exchange rates—that they seriously inhibit *domestic* trade (that is, GNP).

Since early 1973 flexible exchange rates have gained the upper hand. But the advocates of fixed rates have not given up the fight by any means; they are waiting in the wings, hoping that floating rates sink so that fixed rates can surface once again.

20

FIXED VERSUS

FLOATING EXCHANGE RATES

From the end of Word War II until 1973, the world's international financial system was based on *fixed* exchange rates. When you spent a weekend in Amsterdam or a spring vacation in Rio, you knew before you started what the price of foreign money would be. Nowadays exchange rates *float*, and you're never sure how much it will cost to buy the money you'll need when you get there.

Fixed exchange rates have undeniable benefits. Within the United States, for example, a dollar costs a dollar no matter what state you're in. A common currency within a country is a domestic fixed exchange rate system and it has obvious advantages. It would be a mess if we had domestic floating rates—if dollars were stamped with each state's name on the top and had to be exchanged for a differently stamped dollar, at unpredictable cost, every time you went from one part of the country to another.

Since fixed exchange rates are good at home, why not internationally? On the basis of such thinking, the major countries agreed in 1944 to establish the International Monetary Fund to supervise fixed exchange rates. The fixed exchange rate system worked tolerably well for two decades, but intermittently produced international financial crises that eventually brought the whole system tumbling down.

How Fixed Rates Were Maintained

Remember how floating exchange rates operate? When a country runs a balance of payments deficit, its money *depreciates* relative to other monies; its outflows of funds exceed inflows, pumping too much of its own money abroad, and this burgeoning supply leads to a decline in its relative value. In turn, this relative depreciation of its money should expand the deficit country's exports, contract its imports, and thereby restore its balance of payments to equilibrium.

But with fixed exchange rates, as they existed from the end of World War II until 1973, the process never got off the ground. By international agreement (under the IMF), a deficit country that saw its money start to depreciate had to promptly step in to stop the decline. It did so by buying up its own money in order to mop up the excess supply. However, it couldn't buy up its own money by offering more of the same in exchange—which, as a government, it could simply print—because that's what people were *selling,* not buying. It had to use *other* money to buy up its own, and this other money is called its international reserves.

Traditionally, international reserves have been held in the form of gold, because of its general acceptability. Since the end of World War II, however, most foreign countries have held a substantial portion of their reserves in the form of U.S. dollars, which generally have been just about as acceptable as gold in making international payments. They also hold other kinds of "foreign exchange" among their reserves (pounds, marks, francs, and so on) but mostly they hold U.S. dollars. Other nations acquire dollars when we run our deficits and then hold them as their reserves.

In general, countries use their reserves in the same way individuals and business use their cash balances to bridge temporary gaps between the receipt and expenditure of funds, to tide them over periods when inflows of funds are slack, and to meet unexpected or emergency needs. In particular, with a system of fixed exchange rates, countries also used reserves to intervene in foreign exchange markets whenever the value of their money threatened to slide away from par (its agreed-upon fixed value). A foreign country generally used U.S. dollars for this purpose, paying out dollars to buy up any excess supply of its own money, thereby preventing its own money from depreciating relative to other monies. Or, if it was a surplus rather than a deficit country, selling its own money to keep it from appreciating relative to others.

This means, by the way, that since dollars are the reserves of foreign countries, the United States was in the unique position of not having to intervene itself to keep *its* money from changing in value relative to other monies. All other countries were intervening to keep their monies from changing in value relative to the dollar, and this prevented the dollar from changing relative to them. Read that again to make sure you are still with us.

Now let us see how things used to work and watch a mini-crisis develop under a system of fixed exchange rates. A deficit foreign country—Great Britain, for example—seeing its money start to depreciate, promptly steps in to maintain the par value of the pound by paying out its reserves to buy up excess pounds. *But what if Great Britain continues to run payments deficits?* Then it must continue to shell out reserves to absorb pounds. However, its reserves are far from infinite. Sooner or later, when it runs out of reserves, its "defense of the pound" must come to a halt. When the authorities sense that propping up the exchange value of the pound is becoming too costly in terms of the drain on reserves, and no end appears in sight, *then,* having stopped defending the pound, they start attacking the IMF—to win a decrease in the exchange rate. Great Britain devalues the pound, that is, it lowers the par value of the pound.

Once the financial community senses that devaluation is a possibility, however remote, it is likely to undertake actions that increase the probability of its occurrence. To illustrate with the same hypothetical example: Anyone who owns pounds (or liquid assets payable in pounds) and suspects that the pound may be devalued would be inclined to get out of pounds and into some other kind of money—say West German marks or Swiss francs—until the devaluation has been completed; then, with the same marks or francs, he could buy back more pounds than he originally had. Such "speculative" sales of pounds by private holders must of course also be purchased by the British monetary authorities, as they try to prevent the pound from depreciating below par. This puts an added strain on their reserves, thereby increasing the likelihood of devaluation, which in turn stimulates renewed "speculative" activity. "Keeping the faith" under such circumstances is all but impossible.

International transfers of short-term funds stemming from fears of devaluation can feed on themselves in this fashion and rapidly build up to the point where they generate massive reserve drains. Since devaluations are an ever-present fact of life under a fixed exchange rate system,

countries with balance of payments deficits have traditionally been viewed with some suspicion by those who manage
large pools of mobile funds—treasurers of multinational
corporations, bankers, Arab oil sheiks, financial consultants
to private investors, and others with similar responsibilities.
Indeed, fund managers often got nervous about holding a
country's money as soon as that country's rate of inflation
exceeded that of other countries, since this was taken as an
early warning signal of future devaluation (a rise in prices
that is more rapid than elsewhere hurts exports, encourages
imports, and thereby invites balance of payments deficits).

All of this at least produced a convenient by-product for
the monetary authorities *after* they devalued: they could
always blame the devaluation on "the unprincipled specula-
tors in foreign exchange who mounted a disloyal attack on
the [pound] and finally, despite a staunch defense, succeeded
in bringing it to its knees."

There always has to be a scapegoat!

Floating Rates: Success or Failure?

Have floating exchange rates been a success? In some re-
spects they undoubtedly have been an improvement over
fixed rates. Had fixed rates still been in existence late in 1973,
for example, it is not hard to imagine the financial crises of
vast proportions that would have exploded when the Organization of Petroleum Exporting Countries (OPEC) announced a fourfold increase in oil prices. Floating rates have

STEVENSON

"OK. The forward rate for marks rose in March and April, combined
with a sharp increase in German reserves and heavy borrowing in the Euro-
dollar market, while United States liquid reserves had dropped to fourteen
billion dollars, causing speculation that the mark might rise and encouraging conversion on a large scale. Now do you understand?"

Drawing by Stevenson; © 1972 The New Yorker Magazine, Inc.

absorbed the shocks of that and similar episodes remarkably well.

But floating rates have nevertheless fallen far short of expectations. For one thing, they have not wiped out our chronic balance of payments deficit. If there was anything floating rates were expected to do, it was to rectify that situation by making our imports more expensive and our exports more competitive. But in fact our payments deficit has not really responded.

There are several explanations for this unhappy state of affairs, none of them entirely satisfactory. One is that the balance of payments corrective process takes time—that although the payments deficit may get worse for a while in response to depreciation, eventually it will get better. Economists often refer to this as a J-curve phenomenon: At first things deteriorate, but at some point they turn around and improve dramatically. Things get worse initially because imports are resistant to the price increases caused by the depreciation of the dollar, implying that imports actually rise in dollar volume in the short run; similarly, it takes time before exports are stimulated. In the short run, therefore, the depreciation of the dollar is likely to enlarge the balance of payments deficit rather than contract it. *Eventually*, however, there will be a meaningful turn-around.

An alternate explanation is that we have never really given floating rates a sufficient chance to float freely so they could produce their results. Instead, nations have continuously intervened in foreign exchange markets, nudging exchange rates higher or lower, refusing to let the free market operate. Instead of "clean" floats, we have had managed or "dirty" floats.

So far, then, the verdict is mixed. Floating foreign exchange rates are neither a clear success nor an unmitigated disaster. Everything considered, they have probably been an improvement over fixed rates since they came into being in 1973. Many bankers and business executives would still prefer to return to fixed rates, but the likelihood appears slim that it will happen in the near future.

21

WHAT ABOUT GOLD?

Once upon a time, long ago and far away, the natives of a small island in a remote part of the world had a monetary system of which they were extremely proud. Although they lacked commercial banks and had no Federal Reserve, they had something many people consider much more important —a monetary standard. It was not a gold standard, but it was somewhat similar. It was a rock standard. Near the southeastern edge of the island, on a high cliff, sat a handsome and enormous rock, awesome to behold and thrilling to touch, and it was this that they decided should serve as "backing" for their money.

Naturally, the rock was too heavy, and indeed too valuable, to use as an actual means of payment. Instead, for circulating media itself, corresponding to our coins and dollar bills, they used special clamshells. People had confidence in these because boldly inscribed on them were the words:

Will Pay to the Bearer on Demand One Dollar in Rock

The very fact that this statement was made meant that no one ever demanded any rock. The assurance that it was there was sufficient.

For many years all went well. The economy was simple but prosperous, and those from the Great Civilizations across the sea who occasionally visited the island marveled at its stability and its thriving commerce. The natives were not reluctant to explain the reasons for their prosperity: hard work, thrift, clean living, and, above all, sound money. Sound as a rock.

Unfortunately, one night a severe storm struck the island. The inhabitants awoke the next morning to find the rock gone, evidently hurled into the sea by the furies of nature. Consternation! Panic! Luckily, however, they were saved from the potential consequences—worthless money and economic collapse—by an accident of fate that took place within the week. One of the younger natives, a child of no more than eight, perched on the very cliff where the rock had once been, was looking at a rainbow arching far out over the horizon. Following it down, he suddenly saw, or thought he saw, the rock, fathoms deep, under the water.

After much excitement, it was finally ascertained that on very clear days, when the sea was calm and the sun at a certain angle, some who had especially strong eyes could see it. Those who could not, which included almost everyone, were assured by those who could that the outlines of the boulder were indeed discernible. And so, the backing still there, confidence in the money was restored, and in a short while the island became more prosperous than ever.

Of course, all the outstanding clamshells had to be called in, so that the elders of the community could strike out the words:

Will Pay to the Bearer on Demand One Dollar in Rock

In their place was painstakingly inscribed:

*Will Pay to the Bearer on Demand One Dollar
in Lawful Money*

"Then it's agreed. Until the dollar firms up, we let the clamshell float."

Drawing by Ed Fisher; © 1971 *The New Yorker Magazine, Inc.*

Now if anyone brought in a clamshell to be redeemed, it would simply be exchanged for another clamshell. As it turned out, however, no one bothered. After all, with the backing assuredly there, the money obviously was as good as rock.

Gold and the Dollar

Our own monetary system, of course, has always been much more rational. Until the early 1930s all of our money was redeemable in gold at the United States Treasury. Every dollar bill, and for that matter every checking deposit as well, actually or implicitly bore the following inscription:

The United States of America
Will Pay to the Bearer on Demand One Dollar in Gold

Then overnight, in 1933, it was declared illegal for anyone in this country to own or possess gold, except for industrial or numismatic purposes. Gold ownership by Americans was made illegal by an Executive Order issued by President Franklin D. Roosevelt on 5 April 1933. The prohibition was formalized by the Gold Reserve Act of 1934. Accordingly, the inscription on the currency was solemnly, officially, and duly altered to:

The United States of America
Will Pay to the Bearer on Demand One Dollar
in Lawful Money

In 1947 a literal-minded citizen of Cleveland, A. F. Davis, sent the Treasury a $10 bill and respectfully requested, in exchange, the promised $10 in "lawful money." He received back, by return mail, two $5 bills.

Seventeen years later, in 1964, the venerable inscription was finally removed from our currency. All that remains is an unpretentious observation: "This note is legal tender for all debts, public and private." Also (in considerably larger print): "In God We Trust."

Pursuing the same theme somewhat further, until 1965 the Federal Reserve was required to hold reserves in the form of warehouse receipts for gold, called gold certificates. The amounts required were 25 percent behind bank deposits at the Federal Reserve banks (bank reserves) and also 25 percent behind all outstanding Federal Reserve Notes (most of our currency). These gold certificate reserves were considered the ultimate backing behind our money, both checking accounts and currency. Indeed, economics textbooks were fond of portraying our monetary system as an inverted pyramid, with a base of gold that supported an equal volume of gold certificates, above that a fourfold expansion of checking bank reserves and currency, and atop that a further multiple expansion of checking deposits. It was clear to any conscientious reader that without its Atlas-like foundation of gold the entire U.S. monetary system would collapse.

But then, as the U.S. gold stock dwindled from over $20 billion in 1958 to less than $16 billion at the end of 1964, the gold backing behind bank deposits at the Fed was quietly eliminated by Congress and the president on 3 March 1965. Three years later, on 19 March 1968, the corresponding gold reserve against currency was also abolished, just as casually. No one seemed to care. The newspapers hardly mentioned it. Was somebody covering up?

All of which raises an intriguing question. There is, we are told, billions of dollars worth of gold buried deep beneath the surface of the earth in heavily guarded Fort Knox, Kentucky. Have you ever seen it? Do you know anyone who has?

Why don't you write a letter to the Federal Reserve or the Treasury, tell them you're going to be in Kentucky anyway, and ask them to let you stop by and take a look at the gold in Fort Knox? On second thought, don't bother. We did and got back a rather chilly reply: "With reference to your inquiry relating to Fort Knox, all the gold is stored in sealed compartments and no visitors are allowed."

Sealed compartments? No visitors allowed? It sounds more like King Tut's tomb or Count Dracula's crypt than a twentieth-century monetary system. A curse on all who shall enter here! Do you *really* believe there is any gold there? Does it really matter?

Is Gold a Good Investment?

Although we have broken free from our superstitious attachment to gold here at home, it is highly unlikely that gold will soon disappear from the world monetary stage. Thus the question naturally arises: Is gold an attractive investment? Is buying gold a wise way to get rich or a dumb way to go broke?

Because gold earns no interest or dividends, it immediately suffers in comparison with such alternatives as savings accounts, bonds, stocks, and rental property—although in this respect it is similar to diamonds, stamps, rare coins, art objects, and nonincome-producing real estate. Because it yields no current income, the wisdom of buying gold thus depends entirely on the prospect for future price appreciation.

If gold can be expected to rise in price by more than about 5 to 10 percent annually, which is roughly what one can earn in a savings account or in bonds or stocks, then it is worth considering seriously as an investment. But if it is not likely to match that rate of price appreciation, one can do better —and with greater safety—in one of the more customary forms of investment. In terms of this criterion, the historical record indicates that there have been only three periods in the past hundred years when an investment in gold would have paid off. One was the period just prior to 1934, the second was the period from the end of 1967 to the end of 1974, and the third was from mid-1976 through *early* 1980.

In January of 1934 President Roosevelt increased the price of gold by 69 percent, from $20.67 to $35 an ounce. Thus anyone who had the foresight to buy gold at $20.67 from February of 1929 through February of 1933, and who sold it at $35 in February of 1934, would have been rewarded with a compound rate of return of anywhere between 11 and 70 percent per annum, the exact figure depending on when it was bought. In recent years gold buyers have done even better: the free market price of gold rose from $35 an ounce in 1967 (unchanged since 1934) to a peak of almost $200 in December of 1974, a compound annual rate of price increase close to 30 percent for the entire seven-year period. Indeed, between late 1972 and late 1974 the price of gold more than *tripled!* And from mid-1976 to *early* 1980 it rose from $105 to almost $900 an ounce!

But be careful, because these figures greatly exaggerate the likely profits obtainable from gold in recent years. The free market price did not rise without interruption from 1967 through 1974. During much of 1971, for example, the price was below 1969 levels, and similarly from June through November of 1973 the price of gold fell by 30 percent. Or how do you think people felt who bought gold at $195 an ounce in January of 1975, as soon as ownership by Americans again became legal, and then watched it fall to $105 by

I was born in 1929, when gold was selling for $20.67 an ounce... I married in 1968, in an outwardly happy marriage. That was the year gold began to go up again... For the past few years my wife has been having an affair with another man...

...Six months ago she went off to live with him... If I had bought gold in 1929 I could sell it today at 9 times the price at $180 an ounce, up from $20.67 then... Last week she came back 'To give our marriage another chance,' she says... 'To give our marriage another chance?' I tell her, 'Until next time you leave, you mean'...

Some say gold stocks yes, gold bars no. I say gold bars yes, gold stocks no... Yesterday she left 'forever'... This morning she's back again... 'I want to say something,' she says...

Drawing by Lou Myers; © 1975 *The New Yorker Magazine, Inc.*

July of 1976? That's a 45 percent drop in value in just a year and a half. Not to mention the decline from $875 per ounce in January of 1980 to $490 in March of 1980—only two months later.

Supply and demand factors make the price of gold highly volatile. With respect to supply, new production adds to the existing stockpile at the rate of only about 2 percent a year. This means that the overwhelming element on the supply side is not the amount of current ore production but uncertainty as to how much holders of the existing stockpile might try to unload. For instance, the U.S. Treasury deliberately (and successfully) cracked the price spiral in January of 1975 by selling 750,000 ounces from its gold hoard, and then auctioned off another 500,000 ounces in June 1975. Similarly, at the January 1976 International Monetary Fund meetings in Kingston, Jamaica, the International Monetary Fund agreed to sell 25 million ounces of its gold on the open market and use the proceeds to aid developing countries. Since then there have been periodic sales of gold by both the U.S. Treasury and the International Monetary Fund. In other words, sales by large holders, including the Soviet Union, are always a threat to break the price.

On the demand side, again, a significant portion of the demand for gold is not for current industrial or artistic use but rather is motivated by psychological considerations—in particular, by fear regarding an uncertain social and economic future. Gold has traditionally been thought of as a hedge against inflation; when consumer prices threaten to rise rapidly the private demand for gold expands, but when inflation subsides that demand often vanishes overnight. This sort of demand typically fluctuates erratically on short notice, and rather small changes in supply or demand can produce wide price swings.

Thus gold is a highly speculative investment in which the warning *caveat emptor* is particularly appropriate. Large gains can occasionally be made, but large losses are just as likely on the basis of the historical record over the past hundred years.

It is appropriate to end this chapter as we began, with a story. A man on a sinking ship ran to fetch his gold hoard before jumping overboard. When he landed in the water, the weight of the gold made floating impossible, so down he went. The crucial question is: Did he have the gold, or did the gold have him?

Epilogue

22

IS MONEY BECOMING OBSOLETE?

What might the financial system look like in the year 2000?

Buck Rogers and Flash Gordon are passé, Jules Verne is old hat ("around the world in *eighty* days"), and *1984* draws too close for comfort. The science fiction of yesterday has become the reality of today. An excursion into financial science fiction for the "brave new world" ahead should provide a fitting ending for this book.

The Decline of Checking Accounts

"He spends money," they say, "as though it's going out of fashion." And perhaps money is indeed going out of fashion.

When checkbook money first began to gain popularity in this country, in the nineteenth century, it took decades before people finally realized what was happening. For a long time checking accounts were not even considered part of the money supply. They were viewed as proxies or substitutes for "real" money, namely hard cash. Somewhere in the vaults of the banks, it was thought, nestled the coin and currency, dollar for dollar, behind every checking account.

As a matter of fact, even coin and currency were suspect. Dimes and dollar bills were considered mere stand-ins for the

really genuine article—gold coin or bullion. That, and only
that, was truly money. Anything less was, like Daylight
Saving Time, a violation of the Lord's will.

Today, checks are gradually losing their monetary importance, just as currency did a century ago. Checking accounts
still constitute the bulk of our money supply, but the money
supply itself has been diminishing in importance in our
evolving financial system. Thirty years ago the money supply, currency plus checking accounts, amounted to half of
our gross national product. Twenty years ago it was equal to
around a third of GNP. Today it has shrunk to less than
one-sixth of GNP. We are carrying on more and more business, both financial and nonfinancial, with a relatively
smaller and smaller supply of money.

Just as a hundred years ago coin and currency gradually
gave way to the convenience and efficiency of checking accounts, so today checks, as we have known them, are gradually giving way to even more convenient and efficient payment mechanisms. The growth of credit cards, for example,
has made it unnecessary to write twenty-five checks when
making twenty-five purchases. One check, at the end of the
month, will do for all. And often that one check is not even
needed. Your friendly neighborhood bank can make an automatic debit to your account at regular intervals, relieving you
of the need to write even that one check.

If you have your paycheck sent directly to your bank by
your employer and make most of your purchases with that
bank's credit card, with payment then settled up at stated
intervals by the bank automatically reducing your account
by the amount of the charges incurred, you will soon find
your check book obsolete.

If we combine the essence of this already realistic payments system with the potentialities of the high-speed com-

puter, magnetic tape storage, remote feed-ins, and satellite transmission, it does not take too much imagination to make a stab at the shape of things to come.

Debits and Credits in the Year 2000

A few decades from now, coins will probably still be with us for inserting into vending machines that we can then shake and bang to release our aggressions. But checks may well have vanished as quickly as they came. Check payment is really nothing more than a bookkeeping operation to begin with. As a method of information dispersal as to how the books should be kept, checks are—in light of present and foreseeable technology—notoriously cumbersome, slow, unreliable, and inefficient.

More in keeping with the twenty-first century will be a vast nationwide balance sheet and clearing system in which debits and credits can be rung up virtually instantaneously by electronic impulse. Every individual and every transacting organization of whatever sort will be tagged at birth with a number and a slot on the "books" of a computerized nationwide accounting and payments system, a National Ledger as it were.

Credits and debits to each individual account will be made by the insertion of a twenty-first century version of a credit card into a twenty-first century version of a telephone or teletype. Instead of a written piece of paper instructing a bank to credit this account and debit that one—that is, a check, with its necessary physical routing from place to place —the insertion of a plastic card into the appropriate recepta-

cle will automatically credit and debit both accounts instantaneously. It should not be too difficult to devise a system
whereby the proper code will serve as a means of verifying
the validity of the electronic instructions to the Great Master
Bookkeeper in the Sky.

Eliminating checks would be only one of the many advantages that would emerge from such a system. All financial
assets are nothing more than a representation of someone
else's liability or evidence of equity. Current practice, which
consists of inscribing same on embossed parchment, has been
absurd for at least two generations. There is no need for
stocks and bonds to look like Pronouncements of State by
King Henry VIII. As everyone is fully aware, a simple computer print-out would do just as well. However, by the year
2000 even that will not be necessary, since it will all be
recorded automatically on the magnetic tape of the National
Ledger as soon as a stock or bond is issued or a transaction
made.

An even more important advantage will be the saving in
time and effort currently devoted to keeping the books in a
society slowly but surely being inundated by paperwork. We
are only kidding ourselves if we think we have made much
progress in this area since quill pens replaced whatever it was
they replaced.

In any event, peoplepower will have to be saved somewhere to provide personnel for the army of computer repairpeople who will in all certainty be busy around the clock
answering customer complaints and fixing breakdowns in the
equipment. One supply source for repairpeople, of course,
will be the cadres presently known as the Monetarists and
the Keynesians. Their hard-learned skills will be obsolete in
the twenty-first century. After spending a lifetime ac-
cumulating correlation coefficients designed to test the role

of money in economic activity, what else will they be able to do when money itself becomes no more than a historical *curiosa?*

A National Ledger payments system will be possible in a surprisingly few years. Already its introduction depends more on costs and financial evaluations regarding its profitability than on purely technological considerations. It remains to be seen whether the necessary services will be provided by one firm, by an association of private financial and nonfinancial firms, or by the government, alone or in partnership with private enterprise.

Implications for Financial Markets

With methods of communication and the dissemination of information perfected to the ultimate degree by the year 2000, in all likelihood financial markets will finally take on the characteristics of the purely competitive markets that economists have been talking about in classrooms since the days of Adam Smith. Instead of simple buy and sell orders, or bid and offered quotations, potential buyers and sellers of financial assets will be able electronically to transmit complete demand and supply schedules to a central clearing computer, specifying the amounts of various securities they wish to buy or sell at a range of alternative prices.

Of course, this in itself would not be quite sufficient to meet classroom standards for a purely competitive market, since one of the prerequisities for such a market is that the participants possess perfect foresight regarding the future as well as perfect knowledge of the present. But even that might be incorporated by feeding probability forecasts into the Giant Maw of the computer. Is it too farfetched to suggest that such forecasts might even involve some of the parapsychological techniques, like clairvoyance and precognition, currently under intensive study at some of our most prestigious universities and on several all-night radio programs?

Implications for the Economy

Economic policy making, Monetarist or Keynesian, will also mean something quite different in the twenty-first century from what it means today. Monetary and fiscal policy are far too uncertain in their impact for use in the Century of Efficiency that will follow the present Century of Progress.

By that time, all assets and liabilities as recorded on the National Ledger will be subject to increase or decrease by any given percentage by Executive Order, thereby instantaneously altering the wealth of every individual and every business firm in the country. If aggregate spending does not respond promptly in the direction and amount desired, further asset-valuation adjustments can be fine-tuned until the reaction on the part of the private sector conforms to what is deemed necessary to assure the Good Life for all.

Given human nature, this may possibly give rise to the problem of "valuation evasion"—that is, an illegal market in which assets are valued and transactions effected at prices other than those recorded on the National Ledger. The result would be the accumulation of unrecorded wealth for those involved in such dealings. If this gains currency, so to speak, an entire underground financial system—complete with (unreported) deposits, handwritten checks, and a subterranean check-routing network—is likely to spring up in opposition to the more efficient computerized and satellite-supervised official payments system.

The most effective remedy to prevent such undermining of the common welfare would be to bar all participants in Financial Subversion from access to the National Ledger. Practitioners of too-private enterprise would thus be consigned to deserved financial ostracism as Subverters of the National Happiness.

Such a solution would have the self-evident virtue of safeguarding the Sinews of our Efficiency, while at the same time being consistent with the preservation of our Cherished Freedoms.

SELECTED READINGS

Data and Current Comment

A comprehensive source of information on current monetary data, credit conditions, general economic trends, and the policies of the central bank is the *Federal Reserve Bulletin,* published monthly by the Board of Governors of the Federal Reserve System. However, more sparkling comment and analyses are generally found in the monthly reviews of the various Federal Reserve banks. Each of these banks will put you on its mailing list without charge if you drop a postcard to its Public Relations Department.

Also well worth reading are the annual *Economic Report of the President* and the publications of several private financial institutions, most notably Morgan Guaranty Trust Company's monthly *Survey,* Citibank's *Monthly Economic Letter,* and the Bankers Trust Company's annual *Credit and Capital Markets.* The main offices of all three of these banks are in New York City.

Books on Money and Policy

If you can still stand us after what you've been through, a basic money and banking textbook that goes into all this in more detail is Ritter and Silber, *Principles of Money, Banking, and Financial Markets,* 4th edition (Basic Books, 1983).

A highly recommended advanced work is Milton Friedman and Anna J. Schwartz, *Monetary Trends in the United States and the United Kingdom, 1867-1975* (Chicago: University of Chicago Press, 1982).

A convenient summary of Milton Friedman's views on monetary issues can be found in his *A Program for Monetary Stability* (New York: Fordham University Press, 1960). Keynesian ideas all stem, of course, from John Maynard Keynes, *The General Theory of Employment, Interest, and Money* (New York: Harcourt, Brace and World, 1936).

INDEX